PERSPECTIVE AFFECTS EVERYTHING

Wisdom One-liners Guaranteed to Change Your Thinking

PERSPECTIVE AFFECTS EVƎꓴ⅄THIⴹↃ

*Wisdom One-liners Guaranteed
to Change Your Thinking*

By
DR. KEITH W. EBLE
CLINICAL PSYCHOLOGIST

Publishing, composition, and design managed by Niche Pressworks

www.nichepressworks.com

ISBN: 978-1541170469

FOREWORD

As a cognitive-behavioral therapist for many years, I am more convinced than ever that **our minds are much more powerful** than we have ever realized. Strong proponents of this idea like Norman Vincent Peale and Steven Hawking have been encouraging us to be more aware of this power in all of us, and then to use this ability more fully. In particular, I believe every event in our life is filtered through and acted upon by our unique viewpoint, or **perspective** – *often without our awareness*. This perspective forms the basis for determining what each event means to us, even before we respond or act; in fact, our perspective determines our action. The more we can be aware of this fact, the more "in charge" of our lives we are and the more intentional our behavior can be. We can better protect ourselves from stress, emotional negativity, demands of work or society, and unhealthy relationships. Not only can we live better individually, but we can interact with others in more positive, peaceful, encouraging ways.

This may sound impossible, but I believe strongly it can be done. This book holds many bits of wisdom about **our perspective** drawn from my experience as a therapist. Over the years, I found myself repeating advice to many of my clients, often in a brief, easily remembered statements. When I began writing them down, I had only a handful, but as I borrowed ideas from wiser people than myself, and as clients contributed their own one-liners, and as I created others, the list grew. At some point, my realization these might be valuable to others became a new driving force for me. As I continued to create and collect ideas and as the list grew, I became more convinced all these ideas could be very helpful to others – thus, this book.

My intent is these wisdom one-liners will appeal to everyone who is interested in growing emotionally. I strongly believe they will fit with any theoretical orientation in psychology, but they are more inclined toward a cognitive-behavioral approach. I also see these as aligned with common sense, another reason I believe they will be useful to many who seek growth.

I mentioned many of the bits of wisdom are borrowed. I have attempted to identify the original creator of each one whenever possible, but there were times when I found no clear reference. I apologize to anyone who did not get credit for their own gem of wisdom and to anyone whose wisdom was attributed to someone else. I certainly want to thank all the clients who contributed their own original one-liners, which were rich in truth and wit.

As for how best to enjoy this book, I imagined people doing so in many ways. I thought some would read whole chapters, while others might sample a variety of single entries, or some might digest one or two pages at a sitting; there is no right way. Each entry does stand on its own, even though some have a special connection to one or two nearby one-liners; of course, all fit in the theme of the chapter. No matter which way you choose to read, please consider the wisdom, challenge yourself (if desired), utilize the ideas for growth, and most importantly enjoy. Happy reading

ACKNOWLEDGEMENTS

Thank you to everyone who contributed to this book, directly or indirectly. I greatly appreciate those clients who, over the past 33+ years, allowed me to work with them and fine tune these ideas. Through their feedback, questions, points they found interesting or confusing, and their growth, I matured and developed as a therapist and speaker.

So, thanks to my many clients. Some of their wisdom is included in this collection of wisdom one-liners. Several contributed their own memorable statements that contained a special truth; and, they eagerly agreed to let me borrow them to use in the future.

My family contributed in many ways, too, helping me work the kinks out of many of the witticisms you'll find here. They offered support as I persevered in the writing task, and were patient with my absence while I spent hours at the computer. From the beginning, they encouraged me to "Do it! Write the book." They also contributed their time to read, proofread, and offer feedback. My daughter Emily turned my sketches into professional drawings. For all of that, I am extremely grateful.

Thanks go out to the many professionals in the field of psychology, who clearly paved the way for me to find and polish these gems of wisdom. From my formal trainers (professors and supervisors), to colleagues, to master theorists in psychotherapy – thank you for the foundation you provided.

CONTENTS

CHAPTER 1

PERSPECTIVE IN GENERAL

WHAT IS THE BASIS FOR YOUR PERSPECTIVE?

There is an old Indian parable about five blind men asked to describe an elephant, which they had not encountered before. The first man, who was holding the elephant's tail, announced, "An elephant is like a rope." The man feeling the elephant's leg stated, "An elephant is like a tree." The one touching the elephant's side said, "It is like a wall." The man holding the ear exclaimed, "An elephant is like a large fan." The last man, exploring the gently weaving trunk, said abruptly, "An elephant is like a snake." Clearly, their *beliefs* were determined by their *perspectives*. In each case, their perspective was unknowingly limited by limited information. How often do we form beliefs (and responses) based on similar perspectives from limited information, never realizing there is more to the picture?

"MEN ARE DISTURBED NOT BY THINGS, BUT BY THE VIEWS WHICH THEY TAKE OF THEM."
Epictetus, first century AD

"THERE IS NOTHING GOOD OR BAD BUT THINKING MAKES IT SO."
Shakespeare, in Hamlet

IT'S ALL IN YOUR PERSPECTIVE
Like a quote by Marcus Aurelius

Some people believe it is events that cause us to react, and so we all react in the same, predictable ways. For example, if another person steps on my foot, I **automatically** get angry and strike out. That's just life. On the contrary, others realize we are *not* pre-programmed in our responses. Norman Vincent Peale said, "Change your thoughts and you change your world." He would argue how we react depends on how we look at the event or how we interpret the event. For example, a loud noise outside (from an event which we did not observe) could be interpreted as a car backfiring, a large item being dropped, or a gunshot. Since we did not see the cause, we are free to believe whatever we choose. Of course, our physical and emotional reactions are determined by the belief—or *perspective*—we choose, not the truth (which is unknown).

Another example in which *perspective clearly determines our reaction* is a car weaving through traffic. We could ask: is that driver drunk? on a cell phone? a woman in labor? an elderly man going to pick up medications? or just selfish? According to this idea about perspective, what I think determines what I feel and how I react; and, the truth has no bearing on my reaction. Oddly, I will likely *never* know the truth about that other driver. One more example: if your partner gives you a small gift (flowers or candy), is it a nice, thoughtful gesture? or is it an attempted apology for an unknown transgression? or is it an irresponsible expenditure of your limited finances? Your reaction to the gift depends entirely on our *perspective about it*.

You have probably heard the question "Is the cup half full or half empty?" It is rhetorical, because by definition, both are true at the same time. In everyday activities, we typically focus on or emphasize *one half*, which becomes our perspective; it then determines our next reaction. For people who struggle the most in life, their choices are typically negative, creating negative attitudes (perspectives) and responses. Even though we readily acknowledge the situation in front of us is both full (or positive) and empty (negative) at the same time, we often have a bias to see it, or interpret it, as negative. What happened to the other option - the positive – to form my perspective? Well, it is still there, if any of us chose to take it.

The everyday value of realizing how our perception interprets everything allows us to *choose* how we *want to react* to situations. We can change our *interpretation* or *perspective* and completely alter our experience of life, events, and situations. One beautiful and progressive application of this shift would be seeing everyday mistakes as "simply human" (and normal), instead of terrible, awful, catastrophic, or unforgivable. Such a shift in perspective could be huge.

PERSPECTIVE CAN BE A KEY TO HUMOR

A man was sitting on a park bench tearing up some newspaper and throwing it into the wind. A passerby stopped and asked him what he was doing. The man stated, "I'm keeping the elephants away." The passerby emphatically stated, "There are no elephants here," to which the man proudly replied, "You see, it's working." He definitely had his own perspective.

EVENTS HAVE NO MEANING IN AND OF THEMSELVES
Like a quote by Tony Robbins

Have you ever wondered why two people are able to see the same situation so differently? It is simple - we each *choose our own meaning* for every situation. We make it fit our unique history, as well as our needs at the moment. For example, when two people look at the same rain clouds, one might be grateful for the much-needed rain, while the other may be upset that the rain will ruin his picnic. Or, when a young child does not follow all the rules for proper eating in a restaurant, the child could be seen as "acting like a baby" or, more respectfully, as "tired and bored." With every event in our lives, we decide what it means to us, personally. Amazingly, we may go on to believe our meaning is the *truth*, and our meaning is how others should see the event, too.

This applies most notably to memories of past events. When someone is abused as a child, the *meaning* they attach to the events is often "I did something wrong," "I deserved it," or "It was my fault." Why? Likely, that is what they were told. Since they did not have the ability as a child to think differently, they held on to

3

the explanations given them. They may hold those perceptions for many years, not realizing these ideas are wrong, but being affected daily by these perceptions. In order to make changes when they get older, they need to *find new meanings* for those past events: "The adult was wrong," or "I did nothing to deserve that," or "The abuse was clearly the fault of the adult." As long as the original *meaning* persists, the old reactions - self-doubt, damaged goods, bad person, unlovable – persist, too.

EVERYONE HAS A PERSPECTIVE

Three men were sitting on a park bench. One was reaching up and seemed to be pulling something down. The second man was shuffling his hands back and forth, side to side, as if moving something. The third walked his fingers up his arm, over and over. When asked what they were doing, the first man replied, "Picking apples, picking apples." The second man was "Putting them in a basket, putting them in a basket." The third man said, "I'm getting out of here, those two guys are crazy."

CHANGE IS NEITHER POSITIVE NOR NEGATIVE, UNTIL YOU MAKE IT SO
Like a quote by Marcus Aurelius

Like the quote by Shakespeare stated above, we *decide* what is positive or negative, and in our society, people often consider change a bad thing, unless it is carefully planned and fully expected. With any change, we are required to adjust, to adapt, to make room in schedules, or perhaps make room in our houses. Stress is often defined as change, either positive or negative. Since change has no automatic value to it, the value is determined by each one of us. How do we choose to look at change, receive it, and work with it? That depends on our attitude and perspective. As a child, my grandma moved in with us, which meant I had to give up my room, and the bathroom smelled worse, and there were foods we were not supposed to have in the house, because of her diabetes. Still, there were times when Grandma was fun, she knew a lot, and she spoiled us with her hidden stash of sweets. She was also a good listener – sometimes better than either mom or dad – and she never seemed to be in a hurry. Having Grandma move in was certainly a change, but was it a good or a bad change? Today, it depends on what I choose to remember and the *meaning* I attach to it; that gives me my perspective.

How many times has each of us anticipated something would be bad (especially when it was a big change) but later were surprised? We tend to set our perspective firmly—and negatively—ahead of time, and are not open to what actually happens. For most of us, asking for our first date, being in the ninth grade, moving to a new town/subdivision, inviting neighbors over for dinner the first time, or asking for a raise almost automatically start us thinking negatively, expecting a bad result. If we can hold our judgment for a bit, not form a firm perspective, and see how each of these events goes, we will be better off.

IF YOU CAN'T IMAGINE IT—YOU CAN'T ACHIEVE IT
William Arthur Ward

For many, imagination is considered the beginning of the creative process for anything - and everything. Most importantly, without imagination, nothing can be created. Whether we are talking about an electron microscope or a retractable ball-point pen, imagination preceded the actual appearance of each. What does this have to do with perspective? I believe our society has inadequate respect for imagination, and instead, society's usual perspective favors facts, proof, and evidence as clearly more valuable. I believe this perspective about imagination and creativity is extremely valuable to our society, and needs to be honored more than it is. After all, winning a race, learning calculus, building a chair, memorizing a long poem, or being president cannot be achieved, if it cannot first be imagined.

WORRY DOES NOT SOLVE THE PROBLEMS OF THE FUTURE, BUT IT DOES TAKE THE PEACE FROM TODAY
Like a quote by Leo Buscaglia

There is no way to fix anything in the future by worrying about it in this present moment. Still, that does not stop most of us from spending hours trying, hours that involve anxiety, worry, and mental and physical strain. Even more, such time spent trying to fix the future steals time from the present moment, which is the only time any of us have to really do anything. We cannot *clap* in the future (or in the past); we can only *clap* in the present. The only time we can do anything is *now:* like, enjoy family, explore a good book, listen to our favorite music, appreciate the wonders outdoors, learn something new, or show a kindness to another person. "Yesterday is history, tomorrow is a mystery, but today is a gift - that's why they call it the Present." (Coach Don Meyer)

A practical exception to this is planning ahead; time spent today preparing for the future can be beneficial. Keep in mind such planning is *not fixing* anything, only giving us some peace *today* by already having a way to handle a future problem. Remember, too, this problem may never come or may show up differently than we expect. No matter what we plan, this plan does not fix anything in the future, and if we spend time worrying, the worry takes away from today. More specifically, if we are concerned about a relationship, we would do well to give it our attention today. If we are concerned about how our children will learn or mature, again what we do today is better than anything we can plan for later.

GRATITUDE CHANGES MY PERSPECTIVE
Like a quote by Deepak Chopra

In our society, being negative and complaining seems to come easier and be more common than being thankful. If you do have something you want to be grateful about, saying it may be met with a discouraging response. In contrast, there is an unrecognized power in being thankful; with practice, this gratitude changes me, and maybe others. To be grateful, we need to notice good in our lives, which focuses us more on positives, rather than negatives. This shifts our *perspective*, and we see our world – and ourselves – differently. Once we gain experience in doing this, we can even appreciate bits of good in seemingly negative situations. Again, it is up to us, it is all in our perspective.

EXPECTATIONS CAN BE DANGEROUS
Like a quote by Albert Ellis

One specific type of perspective deals with expectations. When we create unreasonable, unrealistic, impossible expectations, we set ourselves up for failure. This results in disappointment, hurt, anger, and even depression. This can happen on a small, every-day scale or with large, major life issues. For example, if my expectation is to squeeze a thirty-minute errand into a twenty-minute opening in my schedule at the last minute, I will surely fail and be late to my next appointment. Or, expecting to remember everything I need from the grocery store - without a list - is a similar set up for failure. On a larger scale, I might tell myself I never had any interest in math or engineering; then, if I decide to choose this as my career anyway – maybe to make my father happy, I have created unreasonable expectations which will quite likely cause me to struggle and fail in my career. It's all due to those unrealistic and unreasonable expectations, setting me up to fail.

WHAT IS YOUR INTERNAL MONOLOGUE?

Our perspective shows up in a significant way with our silent, on-going, and often automatic "internal monologue." In other words, our thoughts. Many of us are not even aware this monologue is occurring or how greatly it affects our behavior, feelings, and other thoughts. It is automatic, because we have been well-trained throughout our life about what we are *supposed* to think. We fall easily into old ruts without noticing we are thinking at all.

How do we change this monologue? First, the automatic thoughts need to be identified and evaluated to determine what thoughts are likely causing feelings we would rather not have, ie the ones causing our emotional pain. Then, with those harmful thoughts, we can **dispute** them, questioning the *truth, accuracy, or helpfulness* of each particular thought. Finally, we can **dismantle** any unwanted thought, gently taking it apart, deleting some parts and modifying others. The result is new thoughts that allow us to feel and function better.

Let's try an example. If I automatically think this will be a bad day (because of the weather, *and* my busy schedule, *and* my boss being back from vacation), most likely my day will be bad. If I recognize my negative thinking, question whether it is accurate or helpful, dispute and dismantle it, and substitute more positive thoughts, I can change my internal monologue and my feelings. This new monologue gives me a good shot at having a good day in spite of weather, schedules, and bosses. In fact, I recommend everyone try noticing and eliminating harmful thoughts.

WATCH OUT FOR THE LABELS YOU USE

We easily throw labels around, perhaps not realizing our emotions react to those brief thoughts, too. A simple example is the label "clumsy," used when we have dropped something on the floor. Because my feelings respond to my thoughts, I would likely *feel*— not clumsy, which is what I *just told myself*—but sad, disappointed, or guilty. Heavier labels show up every day, too. Children taunt another child as "slow," "retarded," "momma's boy," or a host of other negative words. Adults also get into the act, both toward themselves and toward others, using labels such as "company man," "nutcase," "OCD," "schizo," etc. Such labels are powerful in a decidedly negative way.

One particularly harmful example of labels is when parents put negative labels on their own children. Some of these are obvious, such as "lazy," "acting like a baby," or "Why aren't you ... smart ... pretty ... musical ... like your sister?" Some are more subtle, coming about through life events the child had no control over. For example, children often feel responsible for their parents' divorce and no one thinks to tell them otherwise. They may believe their "misbehavior" caused the breakup, and they label and blame themselves for years. As with the abuse example, children in this situation may think "I cried all the time," "I was always sick," or "Maybe I was adopted?" We would all do well to watch our labels and avoid planting negative ideas unwittingly or off-handedly. They can last a lifetime.

HAVING A TRAIN OF THOUGHTS IS OK, JUST DON'T GET ON THE TRAIN

A friend of mine passed along the wonderful one-liner, and I use it often. At various times, most of us have negative and hurtful thoughts. Sometimes the thoughts are destructive, and they can become more potent if we allow ourselves to continue to focus on them. We *can* let these thoughts pass through our mind, and *not* become attached to them. That would be great! Yes, the thought was there, but now it is gone; I decided to let it go. "Some days, life is not worth living," or "He embarrassed me on purpose and is going to pay big time for that," or "I never seem to do anything right" are understandable as fleeting thoughts. I am better off if I avoid dwelling, and "Just don't get on that train."

8

I'M NOT TO BLAME FOR HOW I GOT TO WHERE I AM TODAY. I AM RESPONSIBLE FOR WHERE I GO FROM HERE.

Blame is never helpful. It tends to keep us stuck so we cannot move forward. Letting go of blame is freeing, and allows us to let go of guilt, too. Then we can focus on making good choices for ourselves today and tomorrow. This is taking responsibility for "where I go from here," which is the only choice or decision I have anyway; I can never change the past.

While we do blame ourselves and get stuck, we get just as stuck by blaming others for "how I got to where I am." By doing that, we give away our control and forget we have power to direct our lives however we want. "You don't understand; my mother was so bad to me I will never get over it." If I insist on blaming others in this way, I am lost with no idea how to move forward. Letting go of blame, gives me back my choice - and my power. Now I can decide "where I go from here."

PEOPLE HAVE GOOD REASONS, EVEN FOR THE SILLY THINGS THEY DO

This idea of "good reasons" is a particularly useful one for me. Years ago, a frustrated client told me she had informed her husband – two years before – she was leaving him; but, she was still there. I suggested she had good reasons - powerful, important, and legitimate motives - for staying. She argued there were only good reasons to *leave*. I handed her a pad of paper and a pen, asking her to title the page "Good reasons to be stuck." Next, we brainstormed the *powerful, important, and legitimate reasons* she had for staying, ie being stuck. Initially, she could not think of any. I offered several; then she thought of one. With some prompting and more suggestions, she was able to think of many more on her own.

When we stopped, she had listed twenty-four *good reasons* to stay. I reminded her we guessed what might fit her situation, so we needed to eliminate any that did not fit. She seemed embarrassed as she admitted, "I think there is may be *one* there that does not fit," which is what we found when we evaluated each separate idea. She was surprised there could be twenty-three *good reasons* for her to remain "stuck." We celebrated this new awareness, but I cautioned if she did nothing about the reasons, they would automatically become *excuses*. Then she would surely stay stuck.

When I explained the next phase, she was eager to find ways to eliminate reasons from the list. She chose a reason, considered how to address it and eliminate it, then took action. She continued down the list, eliminating reasons as she went. For example, she was concerned what her mother and mother-in-law would say. When she wrote to them, both were immediately supportive, so those fears (reasons) came off her list. Finances were another concern: could she afford to live on her own? After gathering information about rent, car expenses, food, and utilities, she realized she could handle the money part.

This woman slowly made her way through the list, finding a constructive action for each item. Eventually, she eliminated enough *good reasons* she could finally follow her plan to leave her husband. She was pleased to do that, after failing to make any progress for those several years. I believe had she not seen the good reasons and worked through them, she would be stuck even today.

One way to be kind to yourself is to adopt a *perspective* that includes respect for **good reasons,** like the ones keeping you stuck in a job, a friendship, or a certain role in the family ... or depression. Identifying and "working through good reasons" makes lots of sense, and can end years of being "stuck," as well as relieve frustration and help to open up new directions in your life.

UPS AND DOWNS IN LIFE ARE NORMAL

A myth often heard is life is "smooth sailing." We have been instructed to hold a steady rudder, not be distracted by things along the way, always keep a cool head, <u>and in the end all will be well</u>. This is especially popular in fairy tales, which claim we all live "happily ever after." As most of us know, smooth and steady are not terms that fit much of life. Life is certainly about good times, but also about disappointments, losses, set-backs, cold weather, hot weather - life is full of *ups and downs*. Thinking these are *abnormal* causes frustration and struggle. If our perspective is "Life should be easy or fine," we will believe problems must be our fault.

IT'S NO BIG DEAL

Many of us have a tendency to react strongly to events, interactions, and memories. Those reactions come from our perspectives, and when any perspective is exaggerated or magnified in any way, so is the reaction. For example, if I stub my toe, and start to think "I may not be able to wear my shoes . . . I won't be able to go to work . . . I won't have money to pay my mortgage . . . I will lose my home . . . then I will lose my family . . . I'll live in a cardboard box under the bridge," my emotional reaction will be huge. *But*, if anywhere in that mental monologue I realize "**It's no big deal**," I can save myself much stress and pain - and my toe will probably heal in short order, maybe without missing any work.

A friend told me he took his daughter to the ocean when she was young. She played at the water's edge, but was afraid of the waves, so he encouraged her to see the waves as "no big deal" or "a piece of cake," so she could enjoy the waves. At the time, she was jumping over three-inch waves. As she got older, she was able to continue to enjoy even bigger waves, by seeing them, too, as "no big deal." Now, other, even bigger issues in her life are "no big deal" or "a piece of cake" as well.

WHAT DIFFERENCE WILL THIS MAKE IN A YEAR? ...MONTH? ...WEEK? ...?

One way to help us see an event as "no big deal" is to question what effect the event will have later: "What difference will this make in a year? Or in a month? Even in a week or a day?" This event - which may seem so horrible now – will likely make absolutely *no difference* - even just one hour later. By using this perspective, we can stop dangerous *awfulizing* and feel better emotionally right away. A simple example would be traffic that prevents us from making an appointment on time; as bad as this seems at the moment, it is typically forgotten less than an hour later. Even a temporary disability from a hip surgery (which I had recently) makes <u>no difference</u> three months later.

THIS MAY BE SIMPLE, BUT IT IS NOT EASY
Eric Thomas

Many ideas in life seem simple to understand or grasp. Unfortunately, those same ideas are *not* easy to accomplish, learn,

11

overcome, implement, or remember when we need them. Examples might be losing weight, stopping smoking or drinking, or even jumping out of an airplane with a parachute. Of course, we all have been told how *simple* these are--eat fewer calories, stop buying cigarettes, pour the alcohol down the drain, or step out the door of the plane. However, none of this advice makes these tasks easy. There is no "just" about it.

Why is change so difficult? Most of us say we *are motivated* to get out of a bad relationship, find a decent job, finish our education, stand up to our controlling parent, or overcome our anxiety. So...why don't we? It's simple, right? "Just do it." Well, **it may be *simple*, but it is not *easy*.** The changes discussed here require major shifts in thinking, acting, and feeling. They are definitely possible, but not easy. Changing my own thinking often means overcoming what was passed down from previous generations. Others may try to keep us in those same old, familiar patterns of behavior and relating, because it is easier for *them*. Clearly, there are many reasons why it is "easier said than done."

This does not mean we should give up, but it helps to be realistic about making changes. By knowing change is not easy, we can be sure to collect information about the task before us. We can ask: how have others achieved change? What obstacles have they encountered? What can be gained - or lost - by making these changes? Whose support can I enlist to help me? Are there any books, guides, CDs to help? Would I benefit from a therapist? Knowing all this, it makes sense to do what we can to make this simple task "easier."

IF THIS PROBLEM WERE EASY,
YOU WOULD HAVE FIGURED IT OUT ALREADY

I believe we often delude ourselves about problems in life: we see them as easy and then get upset when we struggle to find the right answers. We consider many problems as "just the way life is," so we expect ourselves to solve these problems easily. Situations like growing up, forming relationships, deciding on the direction for my life – they must be easy, because everyone before us had to deal with them – right? We forget that making decisions or personal changes is difficult; if they were easy, we would not talk about them so much, or read about them so much, or work so hard to achieve them. If they were truly easy, anyone could "figure them out" and show us the way: our barber, hairdresser, bartender, or neighbor.

My clients often struggle with change, and they usually do not allow themselves much wiggle room with this struggle. Many of the rest of us would like to change some of our life-long patterns of thinking, reacting, communicating, feeling, and expecting, in some way or another. Consider that some of our patterns were learned from prominent people who influenced us early in our lives (parents and grandparents), but they may not have had the best skills to model for us. Still, we continued doing what we were taught – or what we observed – without questioning how it worked for them – or now for us. Figuring out what we are doing wrong, where it came from, and how we can respond differently is difficult, and may require high-powered assistance. We may need a new, outside point of view (AA, a good friend, a spouse), with a trained listener and advisor (a minister, therapist, coach), and plenty of time and work to sort out these "not so easy" problems in my life.

WHAT WORKED WELL AT 16, MAY NOT WORK AT 35

Perspectives we hold about our life undoubtedly change over time; hopefully this reflects maturity and wisdom. What once worked well may seem impractical at another point in time. Behaviors which served a valuable purpose at 16 may even be harmful later in life. When this is true, we are well advised to make changes, no matter how difficult those changes might be. For example, I have met people who learned to avoid voicing their opinions or stating their disagreement with their parents, because it was not safe to do so. In their 30s, they realized they were *still* not stating their opinions or feelings, but now it did not serve them so well. With understanding, encouragement, time, and practice, each one was able to make changes. In the process, they were able to appreciate their new voice, as well as to honor the choice they made at 16 - knowing it worked well *then*.

IT IS BETTER TO TRY AND FAIL, THAN TO FAIL TO TRY
Alfred Lord Tennyson

This idea can be a difficult one. Failure in our society represents such a huge negative we may do everything in our power to avoid it. Unfortunately, to avoid failure, we could never attempt anything—

learning tennis, going to college, or starting a relationship. Thomas Edison was supposedly emphatic he did *not* have "ninety-nine failures" (or was it 10,000) inventing the light bulb. He contended he made ninety-nine attempts, which all taught him something and eventually led him to the working light bulb. Unfortunately, fear of failure has been taught and reinforced with most of us, intentionally or accidentally. To overcome this fear requires a new **perspective** allowing failure without embarrassment, guilt, teasing, or loss of self-esteem. A kind of *insulation* from the negatives attached to failing would be beneficial to all of us; then we could try with a reckless abandon, and undoubtedly learn great things.

PEOPLE'S FEAR OF FAILURE IS OFTEN LESS THAN THEIR FEAR OF SUCCESS
Like a quote by Marianne Williamson

While most of us clearly experience the fear of failure, is it possible we also - and maybe even more - have a fear of success? How could this be? When we succeed, others could respond in many ways, with disbelief, accusations, jealousy, or excessive praise, none of which would be comfortable. Another possibility is others might see our success and quickly expect us to succeed again - academically, musically, mechanically, etc. At that point, the pressure is on to produce more, to invent more, or to discover more. On the other hand, if we avoid succeeding in the first place, we can avoid the pressure to perform again. In our own minds, the pressure is off.

TO IMPROVE AT SOMETHING, TRY REHEARSING IT IN YOUR MIND

Many athletes know, as you "mentally go through the motions," your mind can experience such visualization as actual practice. If you practice correctly, your subconscious mind experiences your completion of the task or activity as the same as if it actually happened. This is possible because that area of your brain does not easily distinguish fantasy from reality. To improve your performance and chance of success, rehearse any desired action in your mind. Your brain will think you have performed it. I observed this with a pole vaulter at the Olympics and was amazed to see him go through his movements on a small scale, just like he was about to do them in reality.

WHAT WE RESIST, PERSISTS
Carl Jung

So often, when a problem or personality characteristic causes us discomfort, we try to ignore it, minimize it, or insist it is not important. But, so often, it keeps coming back. This is an interesting fact of life: whatever we resist gets bigger and stays around longer than if we do not resist. One perspective about this suggests this may be a way that we are given multiple opportunities to correct an important, persistent problem situation. If so, dealing with it right away and resolving it quickly means it is likely to go away. An example would be long-standing anger with a co-worker. If we try to push it away, the other person shows up over and over, reminding us about our ongoing, unresolved feelings. Ignoring it doesn't make it go away, it just "persists."

WHAT WE DISLIKE IN OTHERS IS OFTEN A REFLECTION OF SOMETHING WE DO NOT LIKE IN OUR SELF
Marian Keyes

The next time you complain about someone, stop for a moment. Is their behavior one you struggle with, too? Our own weaknesses or problems may cause us to react badly when we see them displayed in another person. The more aware we are of our own issues and the more we work on them, the less the other person's behavior is upsetting - and just the opposite. Consider looking inward the next time you are annoyed by the "ridiculous" actions of another.

THE "WRONG PLACE" AT THE "WRONG TIME"—ARE YOU SURE?

"What a terrible mistake" is the way our society often looks at events that do not turn out the way we wanted or planned. This negative reaction seems both frequent and strong, which assumes that mistakes are a serious problem. Yet, others believe mistakes and accidents are an important part of how we learn and grow. Thoughtful parents may say, "I wish I could save my child the hurt of learning this the hard way, but I believe they just have to do it and learn for themselves." Usually, any lesson we learn from someone else's experience does <u>not</u> stick. However, when we have the experience ourselves, the new information tends to stay with us. One way to look at mistakes, or "being in the wrong place at the wrong time," is: these experiences are a part of our growth and maturation, whether we realize it at the time, or not until much later.

HOPE VS. DEMAND

When we make plans for a special event, we have two options: (1) we can *hope* the weather cooperates and the pieces come together smoothly or (2) we can *demand* everything must go exactly as we have dictated it. Our feelings will be affected differently depending on the belief/words we choose, and the choice is entirely ours. *Hope* implies a desire for a particular outcome, without any requirement everything go our way. On the other hand, *demand* implies much more pressure for everything to work out exactly right. By changing our own word from "demand" to "hope," we can change our belief and lower our stress, allowing us to have a much more positive experience … no matter how things go.

Remember there are often-used synonyms for both "hope" and "demand." *Wish* is a good substitute for hope, as it maintains our desire for low pressure about the situation at hand. If "demand" is replaced by *should, must,* or *have to,* we are likely to create the same high expectations, pressure, and strain.

AND THAT'S A FACT . . . ISN'T IT?

In my experience, facts and beliefs are easily confused. We can hold so tightly to a belief – or have such a strong history with a belief – we become convinced is a **fact.** We defend it, insist on it, and fight for it. In the day of Christopher Columbus, everyone *knew for a fact* the world was flat. There were a variety of theories about what happened at the edge… including falling off or being eaten by monsters … but no one questioned the *fact* the world was flat. Except Columbus. Today, we look at this "fact" humorously, realizing it was a belief nearly everyone accepted.

When I was a child, spacemen in the pretend world of TV were the only ones who had ray guns, and everyone *knew* such guns were make-believe. Today, though, we accept lasers without question. I wonder what "fact" we have today, that will seem silly and bring a chuckle for people fifty years from now.

What does this have to do with psychology? As just noted, we may hold a belief long enough that over time the belief becomes set in our minds and takes on the force of a "fact." As we communicate with others about it, we likely promote our belief as a definite fact, and if challenged, we probably will defend it. In an intimate relationship, this can lead to troubling arguments, and neither person may be clear about the real problem. For example, a husband may brag about thoroughly cleaning the kitchen – a clear fact, while the wife feels frustrated because he forgot to remove the garbage – a clear fact about clean kitchens. Or, an employee might spread the news she overheard that she is getting the corner office – a snippet that turned into a belief then into a fact; she will be quite embarrassed when a different announcement is made the next day – a new fact. One last example: "I have forgotten five big things today; it must be Alzheimer's." This is another belief, that is becoming a fact. As you can see, this unfortunate process can occur entirely within one's own head or between two people; either way it is dangerous.

INSANITY = DOING THE SAME THING OVER AND OVER AGAIN, HOPING THIS TIME, IT WILL TURN OUT DIFFERENTLY
Albert Einstein

This wonderful one-liner is well known in AA. It challenges us to examine how many times have we approached our spouse, neighbor, or co-worker, or an everyday problem or a stressful situation, in exactly the same way, again. We hope finally – *this* time – something will be different. This time the problem will miraculously repair itself. No, probably not. This kind of persistence doesn't work for us, at all. Clearly, our best chance for change is to realize we have a faulty perspective and need to use a totally different approach to solve this problem.

DISTRACTIONS CAN BE VERY VALUABLE

When we face a difficulty in life and find ourselves burned out or totally stumped, using a distraction may be extremely helpful. Unfortunately, many people use these interruptions to run from the problem. Although a distraction does not *solve* anything, a good "time out" can renew our energy, give us success in another area (helping us feel more empowered), or give us time to look at the problem differently. For example, watching a comedy on TV may help us laugh, release pent-up energy, and relax. Then, we are able to address the original problem better.

What are some good distractions? Any activity taking our mind off a problem works. If it also relaxes us, shifts our thinking to a new point of view, or energizes us, it is especially good. Some examples: walking, running, watching TV, reading, writing, talking with a friend, taking a nap, pulling weeds, or starting a project at home we enjoy.

DON'T GIVE AWAY YOUR POWER

Consider a 12-year-old boy with a new basketball. If he takes it to the local court and passes it to a friend, saying, "Let's shoot some hoops," he may have given up his opportunity to do what he wants. In other words, he may have given his power away. Why? His friend could sit on the ball or insist on showing off his dribbling skills. If that happens, the first boy does not get to shoot - he may have given the option away. *Hoping* for another's cooperation or assuming they will do what we want are two ways we give our power away.

In everyday life, we often give our power away by waiting for another person to decide **our** next move: where to go for lunch, who is going to clean the toilet, or what clothes to wear today. We also can give up power by sharing a secret and wondering if they will keep it or telling a coworker our idea for an office improvement while hoping they do not pass it on as their own. In each case, we lost power. We can do this with many decisions, like failing to state a preference about household furniture, never expressing our desires about family size, or being silent when it comes to picking vacation destinations.

TOO SOON OLD, TOO LATE SMART
Gordon Livingston

We all have experienced this idea, even if we have not heard the saying. Hopefully, all of us can appreciate wisdom comes with age. Such wisdom is something none of us had when we were younger, even though many of us thought we knew everything. One way to utilize this one-liner is to seek the advice of seasoned, experienced people, such as grandparents, especially when we are young. When we are older, we can offer wisdom cautiously and only when it is requested. Remember: many young people cannot be told anything, and any value wisdom may have depends on what we do with it.

YOUTH IS WASTED ON THE YOUNG
George Bernard Shaw

When I was 20 years old, I resented this saying. Now, I totally get it. Twenty-year-olds have an energy, enthusiasm, invincibility, and lack of fear, which can be greatly envied. Unfortunately, they often do not realize this for the wonderful potential it is, nor do they have wisdom to serve as an invaluable guide for their eagerness.

THEY SAY MEMORY IS THE FIRST THING TO GO

Of course, they are speaking of old age and dementia; but, memory problems can result from other causes which have nothing to do with dementia. Depression and anxiety often cause memory problems, and, in most cases, both of these can be treated. Other treatable medical problems also affect memory: thyroid issues, diabetes, infections, constipation, and reaction to anesthesia. Stress, lack of sleep, poor nutrition, and dehydration can all cause problems with memory, too. So, there is no need to panic: by changing our perspective, we can consider these other possible causes of forgetfulness, and seek appropriate treatment. Then, we can let go of worry and grief.

ASSUME: (makes an) ASS (out of) U (and) ME

Caution is the watchword when reciting this one. When we *assume*, we often guess wrong, respond incorrectly, then get an unwanted, surprise response. We had it all figured out nicely...but differently. Clearly, this is why assuming is dangerous.

KNOWING IS GOOD, DOING IS BETTER

Our society emphasizes intellectual pursuits and the accumulation of knowledge. Little good comes from knowledge until someone puts it into action. Only *thinking* about being kind or helpful does little good; we must *do* good. With close relationships, we often take it for granted others know we appreciate their kind words, thoughtfulness, or help. We often say and do nothing. Yes, yes, the thought was there, but the expression was not. This occurs with communicating our desires, too: "They know what I'm thinking; I don't have to say it." Yes…we do.

Writing is another activity we are encouraged to do since it is beneficial, but are likely to think about it but not do it. Many professionals in the helping field urge writing, in any form: a journal, a release letter, rambling thoughts, or a feeling book. When we do this, we are likely to *experience* our thoughts moving along a more-or-less straight line; however, *thinking* them often seems circular. Writing to communicate can be valuable, if we *actually do it* instead of simply *thinking* about it! Written communication offers many benefits: multiple chances to get the wording just right, time that is not interrupted, there is no confrontation, and when given to another person, he/she has time to review and respond. Another quite different value of *doing* is that writing passes wisdom on to others, instead of the information being lost when a grandparent, a matriarch, or a family historian dies.

THAT'S JUST MY MAGICAL, MAGNIFYING MIND

A client of mine recently offered this tidbit, originally from AA. I see it as a cute way to remind myself that, first of all, *my mind (my thinking) is powerful*. Because of its power, my mind can solve problems, decide how to feel and respond, and create new things. Unfortunately, my mind can also make interpretations and attach meanings that **magnify** life experiences in negative ways. Often these ways are subtle, so I may not notice the effect. In this process, my thinking **magically** makes my emotions huge - and negative. If only we were better able to magnify the positives in our lives, and increase good feelings and thoughts. Well, it is worth a try. After all, my mind is magical and magnifying.

YOU SEEM TO BE MAKING A MOUNTAIN OUT OF A MOLEHILL

Exaggeration is an amazing thing. With it, we can conjure up great movie scripts or funny jokes to make everyone laugh. Unfortunately, we can also create strong emotions - in ourselves or others - which are difficult to manage. Oddly, many of the emotions are not accurate or helpful, because of the exaggeration involved. Recently, a client announced at the beginning of the session her week was "intolerable." I immediately disagreed, but she insisted her week was definitely "intolerable." Then, I explained she would be dead if her week were truly "intolerable." Did she have a difficult week? Yes, she did, but her exaggeration undoubtedly added to her negative feelings. When we make a situation a "mountain," it makes coping, solving, and even enduring what is in front of us more difficult.

Exaggeration can be dangerous in relationships, too. If exaggeration becomes a deliberate attempt to shift power or blame, it can work, at least for one person. Expressions like "You always," "You never," or "This is the thousandth time," can strengthen one person's advantage. It does not help resolve a problem, however. In this way, my warped **perspective** is not helping others *or* me.

WE ALL COLLECT FACTS WHICH SUPPORT WHAT WE ALREADY BELIEVE

Psychologists call this confirmation bias. As part of our own self-protection, we tend to seek consistency in what we say, believe, and do. To accomplish this, we quietly collect information to fit and support the ideas we already hold; and, we ignore or reject information that does not fit our set beliefs. This may sound self-serving, and it is. The danger is this can blind us to new truths and ideas.

Let's try an example. Imagine two people getting into the same car. The first person says, "I'll bet all the <u>best</u> drivers are out on the highway today." The second person says privately, "I'll bet all the <u>worst</u> drivers are out on the highway today." After an hour of driving, both get out of the car and say the same thing, "See, I was right." Clearly, they both continue to consider their views to be correct, because they unknowingly collected only the evidence supporting their preconceived beliefs. This required throwing away any opposing evidence. For us to avoid this familiar trap and maintain an open-minded approach to life, we need to be aware of this tendency and to strive to collect facts without a bias.

The following one-liners about general perspective require no explanation:

WELL-BEHAVED WOMEN SELDOM MAKE HISTORY
by Laurel Ulrich

21

MOST OF THE TIME, THERE IS NO ONE RIGHT ANSWER

IF IT SOUNDS TOO GOOD TO BE TRUE,
IT PROBABLY IS

IT IS BETTER TO HAVE LOVED AND LOST, THAN
NEVER TO HAVE LOVED AT ALL
by Alfred Lord Tennyson

TODAY IS THE FIRST DAY OF THE REST OF MY LIFE
American Proverb

IF YOU INVEST ENOUGH TIME AND STUDY IN ANY
TOPIC, YOU WILL BECOME AN EXPERT
by Malcomb Gladwell

CHAPTER 2

PERSPECTIVES ABOUT SELF

TRY TO BE THE BEST "YOU" POSSIBLE--BECAUSE NOBODY ELSE CAN

TODAY YOU ARE YOU, THAT IS TRUER THAN TRUE. THERE IS NO ONE ALIVE WHO IS YOUER THAN YOU.
Dr. Seuss

YOU ARE WHAT YOU THINK - GOOD OR BAD
Like a quote by Buddha

This is both an ancient belief and a modern one. It is found in the Bible and other religious books, and it is the basis for some of the most popular current psychotherapy approaches. What we think gets expressed in what we feel, say, do, and don't do; and it may be intentional, or sometimes by mistake, but it works just as well either way.

If we get out of bed believing the day will be bad, it will be: "bad day" becomes not only our focus, but a self-fulfilling prophesy. By putting our thoughts on "bad," we either see everything as bad, or we cause things to go badly, or we actively seek out things which *are* bad. This is where our mind dwells, what we collect as we go through the day, and it is precisely what we find in the end.

Fortunately, the opposite is also true. When we think good or positive thoughts, positive things are drawn to us ... and positive things are what we notice and remember. Clearly, our thoughts become our "day" as well as "the real me."

WHETHER YOU THINK YOU CAN OR THINK YOU CAN'T, YOU ARE RIGHT
Henry Ford

This one-liner continues the idea above: our thoughts say a lot about us. In this case, our thoughts determine whether we succeed or fail. Most of us know when we "put our mind to" something, we are able to accomplish amazing things. Unfortunately, we are just as capable of sabotaging our own efforts when we decide our ideas or plans will *not* work. You see, our minds are equally powerful when used in either direction, creating exactly the outcome we "thought" would happen. As mentioned, any "self-fulfilling prophecy" sets us up perfectly, to pursue the result we have imagined, or have allowed to take shape in our heads. If we think we can accomplish something, we may automatically work hard to prove ourselves correct and accurate, succeeding at our task, even if it takes great effort or numerous tries. If we think we *can't* achieve a goal, we easily give up, offer only half an effort, lose creativity—and prove ourselves right, again.

BOUNDARIES ARE ESSENTIAL TO GOOD SELF-CARE
Like a quote by Brene Brown

The idea of boundaries was popular in the self-help world some years ago. Too bad this idea has lost popularity, because boundaries are a valuable way to take care of ourselves. They are a necessary part of good self-care. As an example, when other people intrude in our life without any resistance from us, we do not do well. We may experience ourselves as manipulated by them, controlled by them, taken for granted, and worse, degraded by them. Without boundaries, others can run over us at will, disregarding what we may want or not want. On the other hand, by insisting on our own limits or boundaries, we can take back control, protect ourselves from negatives, and have an opportunity to make decisions beneficial for ourselves. This is a great way to build a positive feeling inside ourselves.

An interesting example comes from this news report: a new elementary school was finished just in time for the start of school. When the children went out to play at recess, they huddled close to the building, and did not stray far away. Someone noticed there was no fence around the school, and there was a busy highway right next to it. The next summer, a fence was erected. The next school year, when the children went out to play, they hugged the fence. Clearly, they felt safe when they knew where the boundary was; safe enough to go right to it - and push on it.

GIVE YOURSELF PERMISSION

Our society teaches us there are many rules we *must* follow if we want to fit in. There are other rules we *should* obey to be liked by others, be successful, get what we want in life, and generally make a good impression. There are rules we *have to* follow if we want forgiveness, to be saved, or to go to heaven. Unfortunately, all these strong words - must, should, have to - take our choices away, because the choices are already made for us. After all, maybe I *want* to follow all those rules; but, I don't get a chance to decide; this was decided for me - didn't someone say I must?

Permission, in contrast, involves <u>me telling myself *it is ok*</u> - ok to make choices, follow or disregard rules (and be willing to take the consequences), or decide on my own directions. Permission also applies to <u>me letting myself have *all* my feelings</u>, without needing to be strong or tough. An old song lyric says, "…I'll cry if I want to…;" that is permission. And men, crying *is* ok for you, too.

In our society, getting an **"ok" to grieve** can be difficult, from others as well as from ourselves. For example, one common expectation around grief is it lasts a two of weeks; then it is time to get on with life. This is ridiculous. Furthermore, certain feelings – such as anger, relief, or doubt – are often not "permitted" as part of grieving. These expectations about grieving interfere with so many people adequately doing the work of grieving. This shows one particular area where permission is sorely needed, since the commonly accepted "rules" are not reasonable.

On yet another note, some say we aren't allowed to make mistakes, forget things, or be ok with people not liking us. Giving ourselves the go-ahead here – it is ok - is critical for good mental health. Best of all is stopping the pressure of the **shoulds**, since these take away permission from all of us.

IF I DON'T TAKE CARE OF MYSELF, WHO WILL? or I'M IMPORTANT, TOO.

Most of us were taught doing something for ourselves is bad. We were told we should always think of others first and do all we can to "help others." Rarely was there any encouragement to do good things for ourselves or to take care of ourselves. Fortunately, this is changing, with the idea that **self-care** is useful and legitimate. Still, I believe many people today have suffered greatly from a lack of care, especially self-care. Unfortunately, those who suffered did so because they were not allowed to **be important, too**.

To make this change, all of us need to *speak up* for ourselves, by acknowledging what is important to us and *asking* for it. We must believe we have a right to seek what we need, and be a squeaky wheel to assure we get it. Part of this involves an awakening, so all of us will be more aware of what we need, and have the right to ask for it. This means I can, and want to, do what allows me to function to my fullest.

How does this idea fit with the "Me" generation? I would concede there are people who are overly selfish and unreasonable in their pursuit of what they want. There is a generation of people believing they are entitled to . . . everything. Maybe it is because these folks have grown up being given much, so they came to expect they would continue to get much. Oddly, I believe many are not happy, in spite of this. This is not surprising, since many do not actually exhibit good self-care.

An interesting aspect of this one-liner is the "too," as in "I'm important, *too*." There is nothing in this idea that implies others are not important. To the contrary, I believe each of us has a responsibility to honor others and do good for them, to help in what ways we can, and to consider others "important," just like ourselves. To me, this makes sense: to help the world function the best it can – peacefully and compassionately - and to express our appreciation of all we have.

26

SOMETIMES IT IS GOOD TO BE "SELFISH"

As just discussed, most of us were repeatedly instructed to never be selfish, because it is bad. When we are never selfish, we neglect ourselves and fail to show the same kindness to us/me as we do to others. I use this one-liner to shock my clients a bit, by using a "bad" word in a positive way. I believe this allows me to discuss this taboo subject more easily, and help my clients really look at how they take care of themselves. Some of my clients are caregivers for elderly family members, and all their energy goes to caregiving; they do not put any effort into *appropriate self-care.*

LOVE YOUR NEIGHBOR AS YOURSELF
The Bible

Throughout our lives, many of us have formed ideas about "self" from religion. One of the major teachings I recall was "Love your neighbor as yourself" (from the Bible). I think it is fair to say most of us have heard this message many times, and part of the message has been clarified as "Love your neighbor, then yourself." In an interesting article about "self" which I read some time ago, I found a jingle affirming this: "J-O-Y, J-O-Y, J-O-Y spells joy: Jesus first, yourself last, and others in between." I had never heard the jingle, but I clearly got the message; probably you did, too. Once again we have been told not to be selfish. In our society, mothers seem to get hit the hardest with this: they must take care of everyone (else) first. This includes the kids, spouse, parents, and the shut-in neighbor. Then, if there is time left in their day - usually at one or two am - mothers can do something nice for themselves. As long as they feel a little guilty.

Well, if we look closely at this second law of Jesus, it seems it could be accurately expanded to read: "**Love your neighbor <u>in exactly the same way</u> as you love yourself.**" From this new perspective, we need to love ourselves first, to know how to love others. And, loving anyone, including yourself, means to take care of, honor, appreciate, forgive, be kind to, and listen to them/yourself (at the very least). How often do we achieve that with others – or with ourselves? It may help to remember you are one of the people who all of us are to love. It *is* ok for me to take care of me and love myself, too

FORGIVING OTHERS IS MORE FOR MY BENEFIT THAN FOR THEIRS

When we carry a grudge, we are the ones who suffer. It is quite possible the other person knows nothing about our grudge (or does not care) and is not bothered at all. If the other person has died, they definitely are not bothered. In any case, forgiveness is not intended to help the *other* person, as many of us have assumed. The person we still resent might even be surprised if we communicated our forgiveness to them. <u>The real purpose of forgiveness is relieving me</u>: by doing the work of forgiveness - and it *is* work - I feel better, lighter, happier. I lift a burden from my shoulders and release negativity.

How do we forgive? I appreciate the suggestions of a minister friend (Richard Reiger), who said: (1) write down all the feelings to release the energy connected to them (a letter, journal, or scribbles), (2) burn the document, maybe with a "release" ceremony, (3) write the benefits of forgiveness and letting go, and (4) create a way or idea allowing you to move forward, leaving hurt behind. Remember, this act is for your benefit, and the goal is to get resentment and anger off your back.

For those of you who may still focus on the benefit to the other person, that can happen, too. Unfortunately, that person may not believe they did anything wrong and reject any kind of forgiveness. Or, as mentioned, the person may have died or moved away, making them unavailable to respond to your forgiveness. Finally, there will be times when my forgiveness can repair a friendship or family connection, and that can be huge. For the times when no good can come out of forgiveness with the other person, I still can achieve much relief by doing the work of forgiving.

"YOUR OPINION OF ME" . . . IS NONE OF MY BUSINESS.
Like a quote by Tiny Buddha

So often when people criticize us, we take it personally and feel hurt. Well, why not? That was their intent. If we look closer, their well-aimed criticism is their *opinion* about the issue at hand (my clothes, beliefs, accent, or personality). We would do well to remember: **Their opinion of me tells me more about *them* than it does about *me*.** It is their opinion. Nothing more. My opinion about the same issue may be different - and I hold my opinion because

28

I like it and feel comfortable with it. Why "your opinion of me" so important? I believe we confuse others' opinions with the truth, thinking they know more than I do. If we consider their opinion is merely what they think, perhaps we can question if it is a "fact," one that means nothing to me. Therefore, it becomes obviously "none of my business".

An example may help. In the past, when someone said my tie was ugly – "Does not go with your shirt," or "No one in their right mind would ever buy such a tie" – my first reaction was embarrassment and guilt. Right away, I took their words for truth, and I wondered how I could make such a terrible mistake. Then I remembered I wore this tie because I like it and believe it goes well with this shirt. What the other person said may be accurate for *them*, but is not true for *me*. Clearly, their opinion was of no interest to me and "none of my business."

SOMETIMES IT IS OK TO BE A CHEERFUL RECEIVER

Most of us have heard, from religion and other sources, it is good to be a cheerful giver. I certainly agree, but would like to explore the opposite side of this. Imagine, for a moment, 100 cheerful givers prepared with their gifts. To whom do they donate? If there are no cheerful *receivers*, the givers cannot fulfill their desire or instructions. They obviously need people who are receptive or they cannot give. Recipients are necessary in this two-way exchange, and we can cheerfully *make ourselves available for* those gifts: encouragement, a working pen, a hug, a ride, or a new perspective. For many of us, this would be a wonderful positive in our lives.

An example may help. Many years ago, my family was interested in having a piano in the house, to learn to play. I drove by a house where they had a piano sitting on the front porch. I stopped and asked if they wanted to sell it. We talked a bit, and the owner offered to give me the piano for nothing, if I could haul it away. I tried hard to offer him something for it, but he insisted I take it for free. I know he felt good about giving the piano to someone who could use it, but I really struggled to be a cheerful receiver. I am glad I did, because we got lots of great use from that piano.

There is a trick to being a cheerful receiver. As discussed below, we must believe we are worthy of the gift (compliment, assistance,

29

kindness). We know it is easier to be "worthy" of giving, but much harder to think about - or practice - being worthy to receive.

AM I WORTHY?

Interesting but difficult question. We are told, over and over, we fall short, we are not good enough, we did not work hard enough, we did not earn a particular right, or we are second class citizens. Many have been told, to be worthy, they must earn, find a way to deserve, or find a way to create worthiness. It would be nice to know, as a human being, each of us is worthy.

An everyday situation dealing with worthiness involves accepting a compliment from someone else – pretty simple, right? Do we deserve the compliment? Can we believe it is accurate – does it fit us? Will we be embarrassed if we accept it? Is it really a joke - will other people make fun of us about it? Some time ago, I was visiting a friend's house and our kids were playing well together. I suggested we "catch them being good" and thank them. My friend commented he was impressed and complimented me for the idea. I quickly tried to brush it off as part of my training as a psychologist. Nothing big. His response hit me hard: "What? Are you calling me a liar?" By not feeling worthy of his compliment, I inadvertently rejected what he said. How many of us have done that, rather than simply say, "Thank you"?

At a more complex level, worthiness has to do with various big struggles, such as deserving happiness, being qualified for a job, being receptive to love from another person, or believing I can forgive myself. Unfortunately, many of us are taught we are *un*worthy. From parents, church, cruel classmates, and people unhappy with their own lives, we have heard we are "no good," "weak," "stupid," or "selfish." Overcoming these messages is essential to our self-esteem, which rises or falls right along with our belief we are worthy.

REQUIRING BIG CHANGES SO I CAN LOVE MYSELF -- IS BACKWARD

Many people talk about losing weight so they can finally be proud of themselves, and finally love themselves. Or, they may say they just want to succeed at work, all on their own, so they can really feel good about themselves. In many common-sense ways, this seems to be the right way to achieve changes we want. Unfortunately, this approach does not work. We need to do the *opposite* to get the results we desire. By first loving one's self - no matter what we weigh, how much money we make, where we live, whether we are in a relationship, or how much others like us - is the key to being successful. Then, our ability to make major changes in our lives becomes much easier, more likely to happen, and we are more likely to find the support we need to accomplish it.

A tricky exception to this is knowing when to ask for the help that will enable us find those good feelings about ourselves. Seeing a therapist might be one example. You may believe you do not deserve therapy, because you do not love yourself enough; you avoid taking the plunge. "But, it may not be realistic to start loving myself before I start therapy." My suggestion is to start therapy at any point - either to learn to love yourself or to make major changes because you strongly desire and deserve it. Either way, it is important to trust **you are worth** a therapist's time and effort. You are worth taking time for yourself and setting aside money to get help from another person. **You can handle** constructive criticism. Since the goal is feeling good about yourself, go for *that*, and then allow yourself to make the changes you otherwise could not make.

THERE IS ONLY ONE PERSON I NEED TO BE FULLY HONEST WITH – MYSELF

Honesty is a virtue promoted strongly in our society. However, I believe being completely honest can be dangerous and cause serious problems (hurt feelings, broken relationships, or doubt). I believe it is important to be cautious with honesty. Please know I am not advocating we tell lies, just not the "whole truth" *all* the time. Under normal circumstances, I believe we can be honest about most issues with most people, but not honest with those same people about some things. Knowing with whom and when to trust is valuable, because total honesty can do more harm than good. When I was in high school, a teacher was explaining honesty and "tact" to us. She told us she had been approached at church by a woman wearing an ugly hat, who asked, "What do you think of my new hat?" The teacher's response - to be honest, but no too honest - was, "The color goes well with your eyes."

31

The **one person** to be completely honest with is **me**. Oddly, this sounds easy, but it is not. All of us have learned in life to **wear masks** (see next one-liner) and to **stuff** feelings and ideas. As we cover up parts of who we are so others do not see us clearly, *we* can forget who we are, as well as what we feel, think, or believe. We have started lying to *ourselves*. We lose the truth. For those who have deceived themselves for years, getting honest can be difficult and sometimes painful.

A client I worked with years ago knew she was depressed, but had no idea why. As I got into her history, I realized she had never grieved the death of her son five years before. At the time, she was on bad terms with him, so he was living with his grandparents: he died while living there. She put her own feelings aside and tried hard to support and comfort her parents with their guilt. She also had a mentally-challenged daughter who kept asking where her brother was: another distraction from her own grief work. This woman was the youth leader at her church and found herself counseling the teens in the group about the death of their friend (her son). As a result, she had never started her own grieving. Taking care of others was so important to her, she lost track of her own feelings/grief.

WHAT MASK WILL YOU WEAR TODAY?
Like a quote by Andre Berthiaume

One way we struggle with self-honesty is with the masks we wear. We have all heard: "Joey, if you can't be nice to your sister, at least act like it." "Put on your best look for grandma today." "We need everyone to smile so the picture can be a good one." "We all know you don't like spinach, but you don't have to make such an awful face." Such comments were familiar to many of us as children, and these taught us to keep several "masks" ready, so the masks would be there when we needed them. Putting on a mask can be beneficial, especially if we are not immediately up to the challenge of a given situation or being fully yourself may be harmful to others. For example, if we are called upon to give a difficult report in a big meeting, covering up our anxiety could help us do our best job.

One problem with masks occurs when we use them excessively. Others do not know us or our beliefs, and *we* may forget who we are! There are people who wear masks so much, they are not sure which look is the real "me;" maybe it is another mask. Clearly, if we are always afraid to show ourselves to others, we end up living an imaginary or pretend life. I forget…am I wearing a mask? Years ago, I was impressed with a seasoned therapist where I was getting some training. He was able to complete others' partial sentences with humorous endings, making everyone laugh. He was able to do it over and over, never missing a beat. Once, I found him in his office and complimented him on his amazing ability - he quietly stated, "Unfortunately, no one knows who I really am."

I DON'T NEED TO ANSWER EVERY QUESTION I AM ASKED

As a child, I was instructed I "must" answer any question posed to me. Otherwise, I was being rude or hurting someone's feelings. As an adult, I realized not all questions are reasonable and not all information is necessary to give. I realized I have the right to *decide* the information to share or not to share; it is empowering to me. Besides, some questions are nosy or unnecessarily accusing: "Are you really happy with your wife?" "Are you sure you are telling the truth?" Other questions are designed to embarrass and make us look silly. In many instances, I believe the questions we are asked are none of the other person's business. Bottom line: the best response is not answering at all, saying "I chose not to get into that," or walking away.

I HAVE A RIGHT TO SAY "NO"

This idea of saying "No" is another important right allowing us to exercise self-care. Unfortunately, others can make it difficult. They supposedly have our best interests at heart, but they insist we must answer "Yes," even if we do not want to. If they think we have no right to say "No," they may push hard with their request. Assertiveness training from years ago emphasized: we all have a right to try to get what we want, which may mean saying "No" to others. I guess some of us have lost (or think we never had) this valuable right. In our relationships with a spouse, children, co-workers, bosses, friends, relatives, and neighbors, we need this right to function well. It helps all of us to know we *can* say "No" when we choose.

Not
IT'S ~~ALL~~ ABOUT ME

There are two ways to relate to this accurately corrected saying. First, we undeniably live in a "me" generation: "I want . . . I need . . . I deserve . . ." Many people believe they are *entitled* to get anything they wish. But, because we all share this planet, more and more people are realizing we need to learn to share and take better care of what we have. It is not "all about me" getting everything I want. It's about finding how to live peacefully with others, and to leave a sustainable planet for our children.

The second way to look at this saying is in regard to blame. Many people grow up with the belief all the problems in their lives were *caused* by them. Even today, they may think "bad" stuff happening in the whole world is either *because* of them or is *aimed* at them: "I'm the problem." Fortunately, those beliefs are not true, and changing such ideas can result in relief. It helps greatly to realize "What happens *around* me is <u>not</u> always *about* me."

A simple example could involve being snubbed by someone. From the it's-all-about-me perspective, "They did that to me on purpose," "They must hate me," or "That's a personal insult." The truth may be the other person was preoccupied and they were upset with a colleague or boss; ie, their bad behavior has nothing to do with me. If we do blame ourselves for this attack, then we are likely to struggle unnecessarily with the resulting feelings. Hopefully we can see quickly "It's really *not* about me," because I am not that powerful; if I were, the responsibility and blame could be tremendous. When we see it is *not* about us, we can feel and do much better.

I BELIEVE WHAT I BELIEVE, UNTIL I CHANGE MY MIND
Like a quote by Abraham Lincoln

A friend of mine brought this one-liner to my attention, smiling about the twist at the end. There is an important balance implied here – (1) knowing what we believe and holding tightly to it, and yet (2) being able and willing to change our minds in the face of new information. Any time we are overly stubborn, we lose the opportunity to learn new things and grow from them. In contrast, being flexible to point of being totally uncommitted, limits us, too, by giving us no platform on which to stand. What's best? Believe, and be willing to change.

DON'T BELIEVE EVERYTHING YOU HEAR. . .
or SEE. . . or READ. . . or THINK.
Allan Lokos

I once saw a series of T-shirts – released over several years – cautioning the reader what *not* to believe. The message on each shirt was meaningful to me at that particular time, as the cautions escalated over time. "Don't believe everything you hear" - the first shirt - was easy to grasp. Gossip, hurtful words, and opinions, all fit there. "Don't believe everything you see" - the second shirt - registered easily at the time, especially as I recalled magicians using sleight of hand or expertly "cropped" pictures. Then, I saw "Don't believe everything you read" - third shirt - and again I was in the right place to appreciate the idea (questioning self-serving lies, propaganda, slanted news, and political campaign promises).

Then came the final shirt - "Don't believe everything you think." Wow, perfect timing. I knew I could actually confuse, trick, or upset myself, all by myself. I could insist on something being a "fact" when was only a belief. I came away from these shirts knowing caution is valuable, whether I hear, see, read, or just think. Now, I question everything, and of course, recommend it to my clients!

YOUR BRAIN LISTENS TO WHAT YOUR MOUTH SAYS

Often, we assume what comes out of our mouth is what our brain has diligently decided to say, ie, intentionally so. For the most part, we do voice what we think, and agreeing with this is fairly easy. I would propose that, in our brain, some ideas are only half-formed, vague, and unconfirmed. When we speak those thoughts, they quickly gel and we **hear** them clearly for the first time. They register with our brain as what we "now believe." It has heard the message and accepts it as truth.

An example might be how we convince ourselves an error we made was *inexcusable*. That idea while still in my brain was only half formed; but, now it is out and my brain hears it as the absolute truth. Based on this new truth, I am now likely to be a *jerk* for making an "inexcusable" error. Another example might be reacting to an insult from another person by speaking out, "That's not fair, and you are going to pay for it." Now, my brain, in agreement, must find a way to get even, and may be inclined to strike out impulsively. We have long been cautioned about what comes out of our mouths, now there is another reason for this caution - your brain is listening.

DON'T CONFUSE ME WITH THE FACTS, I HAVE ALREADY MADE UP MY MIND
Roy S. Durstine

When any of us begin to believe we are completely informed, we may tune out, because we do not need more information. We can be so sure of ourselves we refuse to listen to new facts, especially ones disagreeing with our position. Why do many of us reasonable human beings fall into this position? It is easy. Thinking, collecting new information, weighing alternatives, sorting out truth are all difficult tasks. We can avoid all that, by choosing to be close minded.

I WATCHED MYSELF GET ANGRY

This is curious, off-handed comment that shows up from time to time. It raises an interesting question: how many "me's" are there? As I try to understand the human mind, I believe there are different parts, even if these "parts" are theoretical and named primarily to make studying them easier. The idea I can watch myself has some amazing practical applications. In dealing with difficult feelings, one approach is to step out of the feeling and observe it; don't do anything with it, especially don't fix it. Just watch. Often this gives us clarity, as well as an opportunity to lessen it, learn from it, and let it go completely. This idea can help in relationships, too, when we are defending or angrily trying to convince the other person. If we step back and observe, this may give us an insight as to how to handle this interaction more productively. I recommend sometimes we intentionally step back, and "watch ourselves."

WHATEVER WE DWELL ON GROWS
Martin Luther

Dwelling is a powerful word, and a powerful activity. We might dwell on a mistake from the past, or a fear about the future. Maybe it's something someone said, a pain in our big toe, or a TV show we saw last night. By dwelling on any of these, we automatically cause them to get bigger. Since most of what we dwell on are negatives - about finances, relationships, work, or status - what we "grow" is usually depression, guilt, frustration, and other negative feelings.

On the other hand, if we can catch ourselves doing this, we have the choice to stop dwelling on negatives and focus on something peaceful, encouraging, or positive instead. By dwelling on a *positive* thought – a pleasant memory, creative idea, or a kindness done to us (or by us) – positive feelings will grow; the positive thought will have a bigger and bigger influence on how we feel and how we function. The whole idea of the "power of positive thinking" (Norman Vincent Peale) rests on this principle. Maybe a better way to state it is: "Whatever we *choose* to dwell on grows." What are you choosing to be the focus of your thinking?

BRAVERY DOESN'T MEAN YOU ARE NOT AFRAID, IT MEANS YOU ARE AFRAID AND DO IT ANYWAY

My wife was reading a book to our children and came across the word "brave." I was eavesdropping at the time, so I perked up when she offered this definition: "Being brave does not mean you are not afraid, it means you are afraid and do it anyway." I agreed, but was a little surprised at the same time. I had not thought of bravery that way. Now I fully agree. If you are not afraid, there is no need for bravery; bravery becomes important only when you *are* afraid. Go ahead, recognize your fear. Then consider being brave about it.

OUR SUBCONSCIOUS CAN HOLD OLD MEMORIES THAT STILL AFFECT US TODAY
Jon Connelly

Most hypnotherapists believe the subconscious is well-intentioned, always wanting what is best for us. But, the basis for the subconscious to determine how to best protect us may come from old, outdated information. An important part of hypnotherapy is to clear any effect of those old memories, by essentially updating them, so the protection intended by the subconscious is accurate for today. For example, as a child you may have been frightened by a big black snake falling right in front of you from a tree. Now, your subconscious may cause you to jump back and withdraw at the sight of any long, black object falling or lying in front of you. Your subconscious is doing its best to protect you, based on your past experience. Clearing the memory with hypnotherapy (or other technique aimed at the subconscious) allows you to approach black objects now, without fear.

WHEN I TRY TO MAKE CHANGES, SOMETHING KEEPS GETTING IN MY WAY

Most of us operate daily within our conscious mind. We are aware of our thinking and actively participate in making plans and decisions. Sometimes, when we want to make a serious change in our lives, we rely on the "thinking part" of our mind to help us; but, the change does not occur. When this happens, it may be helpful to realize there is another part of our brain functioning quietly and independently, often being forgotten: our subconscious. Since this part of us is often ignored, we may not appreciate what it does for us or what effect it has. For example, many theorists believe the subconscious is much bigger than the conscious mind, maybe by a ratio of 85% (subconscious) to 15%. The subconscious is believed to be on duty 24/7, constantly managing breathing, sweating, stomach acid, eye blinks, and dreams.

More to the point, many therapists who work with the subconscious believe it holds old information, and that information may get in the way of the conscious changes we want to make. When I work with clients who report, "Something keeps getting in my way (of change)," I guess the subconscious is stopping the desired change. This is when an approach like hypnotherapy, EMDR, NET, or similar therapy may be most helpful. If "something keeps getting in your way," consider working on changes in your subconscious.

I'M IN A VELVET RUT

A friend of mine suggested not only do we often find ourselves in familiar old ruts, but some of those ruts are so comfortable they seem "velvet lined." I find, when the pressure mounts, it is easy to slip into old habits and old coping strategies. The velvet ruts are handy and familiar, and the slipping happens even though we have learned new and better strategies—they are just not as familiar. If you find yourself going back to an old, less-than-helpful coping strategy, forgive yourself for being lured into the cozy, warm, velvet rut. Look for a newer, better-working way to cope, and gently urge yourself to try it again; soon, it will be the most familiar coping strategy.

YOUR PRIORITIES ARE WHERE YOU SPEND YOUR TIME

Several years ago, someone mentioned this idea to me, and I decided right then to take a close look at my life. I did not like what I found, because after work and sleep, what I spent the most time doing was watching TV. At the time, I would have never considered TV a "priority." I was surprised I was doing so little of other things I professed to love - woodworking, reading, watching the ocean, being with friends, playing the guitar, writing music, etc. I realized watching TV is easy to fall into, since it requires no expenditure of energy, and it is designed to grab my attention and entertain. To do something else requires a commitment, a plan, and follow through. It is easier to settle down and watch TV. How about you? Where do you spend the most time? Do you find yourself doing what is easy? Is it what you want to call your priority?

NEVER PUT ALL YOUR EGGS IN ONE BASKET

This expression is familiar to most of us. From a farmer's perspective, if all the eggs are in one basket, and the person carrying the basket trips on the way to the house, it is likely all the eggs would be lost. From a psychological perspective, we may find it easy to rely on one special person, one job, or one particular activity to make us feel good. If this one "basket" is lost, our self-esteem will be in big trouble. The "hole inside" - our self-esteem – will be empty again. On the other hand, if we *fill ourselves* with a variety of supportive, nurturing people or a variety of positive activities, losing *one* is no threat. We can continue feeling good and doing well, in spite of a loss. And *that* is a great relief.

I have met a number of clients who did put all their eggs in one basket. I have noticed that men as a group often rely on knowing the answers to make them feel good about themselves. At some point in their life, they may realize no one can have all the answers, and their self-esteem falters. In a similar way, I have seen a number of women who relied on beauty as their source of feeling good. They were a prom queen in high school, did some modeling as a young adult, but then had a mastectomy or began to notice wrinkles – their beauty was "gone." We are urged to "diversify" with investments, and we need to do the same for what makes us feel good about ourselves.

FAKE IT 'TIL YOU MAKE IT

I remember starting out as a young psychologist and feeling insecure about my ability to help anyone. I was not clear about my "bag of tools," I was vague about the theories I had learned, and I was scared about how to apply the things I thought I did know. A wise supervisor encouraged me to "act like I knew what I was doing" and see how it worked. Although it surprised me, I was able to do it, I connected well with clients, offered helpful ideas, and I remembered – at the right moments – some of the tools I had been taught. For all of us, we may need to "fake it 'til we make it" when it comes to something new or difficult, like giving a speech, taking a part in a play, presenting a report at work, or going on a first date (at 50).

YOU MAY HAVE TO BE SQUEAKY CLEAN

I recall a teenager I was working with a number of years ago. He had been in trouble with the law several times, but now he was trying to stay clear of any trouble. Unfortunately, when there was a problem in his neighborhood, the police usually came to his house first. Sometimes, he was quietly watching TV by himself, but he had no one to verify this story. Several times, the police took him to the station for suspicion, when he could not prove what he said. When he and I talked about what to do, I suggested it may not be enough to be "clean," he needed to be "squeaky clean." This meant he needed to have someone with him to verify his activities, or be in a group, or talk to the guy who hangs out on the corner, etc. He needed to have a good *alibi* all the time, like watching TV with his grandmother at her house. Have you ever had someone who did not trust you and you wanted to be trusted again? Try being squeaky clean. (I know, it can be a pain in the neck.)

INTEGRITY IS DOING THE RIGHT THING, EVEN WHEN NO ONE IS LOOKING
Like a quote by C. S. Lewis

We all have a fairly good idea of what is the right thing to do. However, many of us struggle with doing it in every situation, because the right thing is not always easy. When someone else is present and aware of our behavior, it provides extra motivation for us to act with integrity (unless the other person is pushing for us *not* to do it). On the other hand, when no one is watching, we might be tempted to do what is easy or what is best for us, not necessarily what we know is right. If we want to act with integrity (maybe for no one but our self), we need to do the right thing...even in private.

WHEN WE GET SOMETHING FOR FREE, WE ARE APT TO GIVE IT LITTLE OR NO VALUE

This seems to be part of our human nature: taking for granted those things which come to us easily. Also, when we believe we deserve particular things in our lives, this attitude can come into play and interfere with our appreciation of those things. We might take health, family, friends, or a job as part of our "birthright" and likely fail to feel any gratitude for it. There are many "things" we take for granted, and this applies especially to *free stuff*. For a child, a free teddy bear is not as valuable as one earned by doing chores. As an adult, there are times we borrow a tool or a cup of sugar or a ride to the office. When it is free, it's easy for us to take it for granted and give it little value – and give noting in return. Learning to appreciate everything we receive, even if it is free, would benefit us all.

DAMAGED GOODS

In my years of doing therapy, I have met several people who had low self-esteem. When I learned their histories, I found many were abused as a child and believed they were "damaged goods." Because of this, they believed no one would want them, love them, or chose to be in a relationship with them. One woman, stated, flatly, her husband did not love her - though he claimed he did. She was sure he *could not*, because she knew she was "unlovable." If he insisted he loved her, he was "either lying or stupid," because there was no way she could be loved. This kind of label can stick stubbornly to people, especially those who have been abused; but, it is only a label, not a truth, and can be changed.

RETIREMENT IS HARD WHEN THERE IS NOTHING TO REPLACE WORK

When my grandfather retired, he sat in his rocking chair, smoked his pipe, and read the newspaper. He abruptly stopped his two-mile walk to work each day, as well as his connections with friends at work and his sense of accomplishment from the work he did.

41

Within six months, he had a stroke, and then died within the year. He had nothing to replace his work and all it had meant to him.

Many people fail to plan adequately for retirement, so they become bored or frustrated easily. As with my grandfather, they may also stop any physical activity, so their bodies weaken. To avoid this, it is helpful to begin - before retirement - to have a plan of action. This might include volunteer activities, regular athletic pursuits, clubs, bridge groups, home hobbies, outings with friends, the church choir, a college class, traveling, mentoring a grade school student, political activity, etc. Such planning can greatly enrich the "golden years."

The following one-liners about self perspective need no explanation:

OF ALL THE THINGS I HAVE LOST, I MISS MY MIND THE MOST
Mark Twain

IT'S NOT WHETHER YOU WIN OR LOSE, BUT HOW YOU PLAY THE GAME

Chapter 3

PERSPECTIVES ABOUT OTHERS

BOUNDARIES ARE NECESSARY FOR GOOD RELATIONSHIPS

Boundaries were more in the spotlight some years ago, and today these boundaries are essential for good relationships. Having boundaries is a valuable way we protect ourselves, whether they are physical, mental, or emotional limits we set. If other people intrude, they may excessively influence us, affect our decisions, or undermine our self-esteem, so we lose part of who we are. On the other hand, when we are in a protected space, we can form our own opinions, make our own plans, sort out our own lives, and protect ourselves. Then, when we are ready, we can ask for help from others and let them in on what we want them to know - and only what we want them to know. This way, we can set helpful limits which define what we want from others, such as consultation, help to solve a problem, or support to maneuver through issues in our lives. Boundaries allow us the private space we all need to think, problem solve, and decide for ourselves. A simple example is telling another person we want them to listen and reflect back what we are saying (or not saying), but we do not want them to tell us how to fix anything. A more complex boundary might be telling our spouse we want to speak with our doctor alone.

NOT EVERYONE IS TRUSTWORTHY
Like a quote by Mark Twain

I was in my thirties before I fully realized the impact of something I had been taught as a child: "Don't trust strangers." We were all taught this. But, for me, there was a subtle, second part to this advice which implied I *could trust everyone else*. Only when I was older did I see the problem with this: not everyone else is trustworthy! Trusting everyone had been a source of much hurt and disappointment for me, until I began to question it. As I wrestled with this new idea of not trusting everyone, I realized it can get complicated:

- Some people promise to be trustworthy, but are not.

- Many people are trustworthy with some information, but not with other feelings or ideas.

- Some of those close to us are not trustworthy at all.

I would like to emphasize not being trustworthy does not always mean the other person will gossip; instead, they could laugh at me, one-up me, lecture and criticize, act surprised I have not figured out such an obvious problem yet, etc.

Clearly, there are many ways for others to be untrustworthy, and it can cause considerable pain for the one who is trying to do the trusting. At first, we don't realize the problem is with the other person, so we blame ourselves. As we understand what is happening, we can learn to be careful with whom we share our private and personal thoughts and feelings. We can determine first whether they are worthy of our trust. Deciding that can make a difference in my perspective and in my overall functioning.

YOU GET ONLY ONE CHANCE TO MAKE A FIRST IMPRESSION
Like a quote by Will Rogers

By keeping this in mind, we can make the most of those _first_ meetings, and not miss an important *window of opportunity*. Sometimes we slip, and fail to see how important these opportunities might be. By remembering this idea, we can put our best foot forward and make the best use of any new situation. We can know that, somehow, at a later time, it will be clear how the encounter benefited me.

BEING LOST DEPENDS ON PERSPECTIVE, TOO

A man who was hopelessly lost stopped to ask directions from a farmer sitting on his front porch. The farmer listened to where the man was going and said, "You can go down here to the next house and . . . no, that won't work." "Or, you could go back from where you came to the big red barn and turn right . . . no, that won't work either." The traveler was irritated and exclaimed, "Boy, you sure don't know much." To this, the farmer calmly stated, "Well, at least I'm not lost."

YOU CAN PLEASE SOME OF THE PEOPLE ALL THE TIME
Abe Lincoln

Lincoln gave us a great piece of perspective with this: "You can please some of the people all the time, and all the people some of the time, but you can't please all the people all the time". This is such a great idea to keep in mind when we try to work with or influence others. No matter how good I am - or think I am - there are limits to my effectiveness, and knowing this is a helpful perspective with others. The value of this phrase can be expanded, too, by considering other words to use in place of "please," like "fool," "persuade," "make them laugh," or "get through to." Be realistic and know your limits.

YOU CAN'T COMPLETELY AVOID CONFLICTS WITH OTHERS; THE TRICK IS TO RECOVER QUICKLY

Some couples have told me they never had a fight, maybe in forty years of marriage. Well, I believe this comment most likely means one person has "caved in," and it was probably the same person every time. Aside from such giving in, couples, friends, co-workers, and families cannot avoid conflicts, or at least strong differences of opinion: this is natural due to living/working together. These situations become problems when they are escalated to involve blame, defensiveness, or serious harm (words or actions) or when they are never resolved. I recommend resolving and recovering - as quickly as possible. This may mean letting go of some pride, apologizing, or compromising, any of which is well worth it. If we

45

get into a habit of recovering quickly (minutes instead of days), the relationship will be better. Try it!

"DISCERNMENT" IS A KEY TO COPING WITH PEOPLE

In line with finding who is trustworthy, we may be at a disadvantage in relationships because we have all been told not to judge, belittle, discriminate, or be unfair to other people. This warning has been so strong, we are often afraid to evaluate a situation or a person about any potential negative effect they may have on us. Deciding who is likely to help or hinder us can be valuable, and some evaluation is both necessary and desirable. Examine the situation closely and decide - without judging, blaming, or harming the other person. This is called discernment, a great tool for coping with others.

FOOL ME ONCE SHAME ON YOU -- TWICE, SHAME ON ME
Randall Terry

Here is another familiar saying tying in with discernment. Most of us can be fooled, "sold a bridge," or hurt *once* fairly easily – especially when we trust the other person. When this happens, it is good for us to be on alert. Then, wisdom and discernment can empower us to protect ourselves, by becoming skeptical, cautious, hesitant, or uninterested. After that, we are less likely to fall for a scam a second time. If we *do*, we need to practice applying better discernment and wisdom.

DEADLOCKED? MAKE A DEAL

Whether we are talking about a marriage, a parent-child, or a work relationship, many unresolved issues can be handled by making a deal. This typically means matching something one person wants with something for other person, and agreeing to a "trade off." Similar to compromise, this is based on respect for the other person, so we can honestly make a reasonable deal. For example, a husband might suggest, "Ok, I will go with you to the mall if we can stop on the way home for ten minutes at the auto parts store." If it sounds reasonable to the wife, they can strike a deal. Or, if a teen wants to have the car for Saturday night, parents might ask their son/daughter to wash it before going and pay to fill the gas tank. Reasonable? If so, they have a deal. This can be a calm, respectful way to resolve tricky problems, where both sides get something important to them. Clearly, some creativity can help, too. *The key is to honestly want to find a reasonable solution.*

I TOTALLY BELIEVE WHAT I BELIEVE--AND I GUESS YOU DO, TOO

This is an important part of respect. When two people try to address an issue, it is often an "issue" because they disagree or see it differently, <u>and</u> because they refuse to honor the guideline: "agree to disagree." To resolve their difference, both people likely try to explain and push their point, hoping the other will realize their mistake; and, "my" belief or idea is "right." This strategy seldom works and often creates anger and hurt in the process. What can help in this situation is to see "I only believe what I believe, because it seems true to me." If this is the basis for <u>my</u> belief, maybe you view this issue the same way. Realizing this can help stop the arguing with (or brow-beating) the other person. *Agreeing to disagree* can re-establish respect and focus on a workable solution for both people.

I'M NOT RESPONSIBLE FOR YOUR FEELINGS

A common theme I have found in distressed marriages and other close relationships is, "You don't make me feel loved." This can come in many shapes and sizes: "You're not the giving ... supportive ... attentive . . . warm ...person I first met." Or, "You seem to have forgotten how to wow... impress ... calm ... inspire ... excite ... me, like you used to." The focus is always on **what *you* need to do for *me***, rather than what we can share together or what we choose to do for each other. In our *gimme* **society,** many people look to others to make them feel better. This will never work, and I strongly urge everyone: avoid accepting *any* responsibility for another person's feelings (even in the midst of love-struck enthusiasm!).

Several years ago, my son described one of his friends as having a "high maintenance" girlfriend. He explained the girl wanted phone calls four to five times a day, no outside activities, and a lot of attention in general. My son mentioned this because he could no longer enjoy hiking or tennis with his friend - he was always expected to entertain or at least accompany his girlfriend. High maintenance is an impossible responsibility and an unworkable perspective.

47

OTHERS' FEELINGS CAN RUB OFF EASILY

Many years ago, my job involved evaluating anyone who walked in off the street to our mental health center. One day, a man came in who seemed in need of medications. I explained the situation to our psychiatrist, and the psychiatrist asked if the man was tense. I admitted he was, but I wondered how the psychiatrist knew. He replied, "Just look at you." Without realizing it, I had begun to feel and act like the person I was evaluating. I believe this can happen in other situations, too, especially in a large group. There is a phenomenon, in groups, where a feeling (often agitation or anger) of one person, is picked up by everyone, and the group takes on that feeling together. With this danger in mind, we would all do well to notice the behavior/feelings of others around us (even if it is just one person we know), check to see how we are responding to it, and ground ourselves in our own desired feelings.

IT OFTEN HELPS TO BE A SQUEAKY WHEEL

We all know about squeaky wheels - they get all the grease. In life, we may need to "squeak" to achieve our goals, ie, make a little noise to be sure to get noticed (and "greased"). To have a good chance at a job, to motivate our investment counselor, to ensure a special person knows we remember them, or to make sure our doctor makes a valuable referral, we may need to be persistent and call several times. If we do not follow-up, we may inadvertently send a message "this" is not important to us. Since everyone is human, the other person's attention will likely go to the most prominent issue in front of *them*.

On my internship, the final position for the year was awarded to the tenth person on the "to call" list. A few applicants with higher ratings had been called and declined, and the rest of the top ten were essentially equal in ability. When the tenth candidate called to check on his status, he was offered the internship position on the spot, and higher numbered applicants never knew.

There is a caution with this idea: too much contact can be negative, ie, pestering. To avoid this, make any follow-up (squeaking) be meaningful: was your complete application received? Is additional information needed? Did you leave your home and cell numbers? When will the decision be made? Or - to be really gutsy - how are things looking, because you have other offers to consider?

ALLOW OTHERS TO DO ALL THEY CAN, UNTIL THEY CAN'T

As people age, they have more difficulty accomplishing what once was easy. At first, this applies to only a few, little things: remembering the name of an object or a person, or opening a jar lid. Later, it encompasses many routine tasks. In a similar way, young children have trouble with simple daily tasks, too. For some of us "helpers," it is tempting to take over, make their lives easier, do the task more quickly, or stop them from struggling. This is *not* helpful. People who have difficulty often *want* to do the tasks themselves. They deserve the respect to let them try, but we can ask if they need or want help. Taking over for them without asking may communicate they are not competent or they are too slow, both of which are demeaning. For the sake of dignity, allow others—elders and toddlers alike—to do all they can, until they can't.

AVOID GIVING UNSOLICITED ADVICE

We human beings typically do not appreciate free advice, particularly before we ask. Although others may see the situation more clearly and can offer a fresh perspective, the person *receiving* the free advice is likely to be defensive. On the other hand, if the one with the advice waits until asked, there is a much better chance the "stuck" person will have a positive response.

CHARISMATIC OR CON ARTIST?

Recently, I was talking with a client who described the man she was dating. He was charming, witty, intelligent, complimentary, kind, and helpful. She was attracted to him, and drawn in by his pleasant personality. But, she was put off by him, too. After checking with friends who knew him, she discovered he was a con-man. Unfortunately, I have talked with people who have fallen in love and married such a person, only to find out much later about their true personality. This raises an important question: how can anyone tell the difference between someone who is "charismatic" and someone who is a gentle, persuasive con artist? The best resource is people who know that person well.

THEY ARE ACTING . . . JUST LIKE THEMSELVES.

Some clients complain on and on about a spouse, family member, neighbor, or a co-worker. They gripe about the other person being inconsiderate or unavailable, forgetting important dates, taking the last cookie, or getting angry about little things. My response is quite consistent: the other person is "acting as you have always described them." In other words, they have always acted this same way - often selfishly. They *are* acting just like themselves. Why is this a surprise? We seem to have this idea that, at our whim or wish, others will automatically stop acting as they have for so long, and become exactly what we want them to be. It is as if we think they will "come to their senses" - or better yet - come to *our* senses. Remarkably, others continue to behave in much the same way as they have before, without ever changing to our liking. They continue to act like themselves.

"YES" LOSES ITS MEANING WITHOUT AN OCCASIONAL "NO"

Parents often want to give their children everything, to make their childhood better than the one they had. This often means the children always hear "Yes" to any request they make. They start assuming the next request will get an automatic "Yes," too. Saying "No" once in a while is good practice, and a good reality check (for the child or for a "spoiled" adult); it helps them appreciate "Yes," more. But, be aware. The spoiled adult or child may react negatively.

I KEPT WAITING FOR "MS. RIGHT;" WHEN SHE ARRIVED, I REALIZED I WAS NOT "MR. RIGHT"

Setting our sights high and hoping is fine, but it also helps to be reasonable with our actual expectations. The girl/guy "of my dreams" undoubtedly is good looking, intelligent, highly motivated, rich, speaks four languages, and has an unbeatable sense of humor. Finding all of that in one person would be a small miracle, but the key question is: would he/she find me attractive, interesting, and a perfect catch? It is ok to dream big and reach high for goals (even seemingly impossible ones), but it helps to keep one foot on the ground.

YOU CANNOT HELP SOMEONE WHO DOES NOT WANT HELP

There is an old light bulb joke about psychologists: "How many psychologists does it take to change a light bulb? . . . Only one, but the bulb has to want to change." No one likes to be forced to do things, especially when they see no need. Change - even for the person's own benefit - often meets with resistance, especially when the change is demanded by an outside source. This is especially true if the courts or high school is making the demand. Another old saying puts it well: "You can lead a horse to water, but you cannot make him drink."

There is an old story about a boy scout who came to a meeting dirty, scratched, and bleeding, with his uniform torn. When the others rushed over and asked him what happened, he stuttered and said, "I was trying to remember what we were taught as Scouts, . . . I was trying do a good deed, . . . trying to help this little old lady across the street . . . but she didn't want to go." Be warned: if you try to force others to change, it could be dangerous!

INTERVENTION CAN BE HELPFUL

There are times when family and friends become concerned about a person who persists in a damaging behavior such as alcoholism or drug abuse. For these times, there is a technique called "intervention," designed to gently confront the person with the concern the other people see, but the person may not admit. This technique involves a gentle touch and a small, select group of caring friends, who offer a careful citing of facts, expressions of genuine concern (not blame), and strong wishes for the person to change. While this approach does work at times and the person agrees to seek help, it is not 100% successful. Some people are quite stubborn and unwilling to admit or face a problem that is obvious to others. This approach can be used for other problems, including other addictions or other "blind spots," like anger issues, video games, tardiness, fluctuating moods. Be aware, this careful, loving, and concerned approach can cause hurt feelings, too.

YOU WANT YOUR KATE AND EDITH, TOO

We are all familiar with the saying: "You want your cake and eat it, too." By twisting the saying just a little, it can fit situations with love relationships. Affairs seem popular in our society, and the people involved often cite the same reason for why they start: "The marriage is ok and I need to stay for the kids, but I need someone who will listen to me." It is no surprise "Edith" can be a great listener, is never judgmental, is always supportive, and completely understands - because there are no routine problems needing to be addressed or otherwise interfering with the relationship.

This idea fits other situations, too, when we want the best of both worlds. We want the job with status, but stay in the job making few demands. We keep the ole clunker of a car, because it is paid for, but we dream about a luxury sports car. We appreciate the convenience of a condo or apartment "close in" to work or night life, but want the sprawling suburban house with the big yard. We want both and cannot be satisfied with whichever choice we make. It sure would be helpful if each of us could make a decision, make the most of it, and stick with that ONE.

ONE-UPSMANSHIP

When I was a child, we often played a game involving this concept. It was based on making insults toward a friend, knowing they would return the favor, then going back and forth to see who could come up with the best put-down or come back. We were predictable back then, though, because we used the same statements over and over. My favorites were: "Your mother wears high-heeled tennis shoes," "Your mother is so fat she can sit on the front porch and back porch at the same time," "You are so ugly your face scares the rats out of the basement," "Your father is so lazy he cannot pick up his own feet." (Sad, when I look at those today.)

In those days it was mostly a game, with no harm done—for the most part. When *adults* play one-upsmanship, the purpose is more harmful and often cruel. With adults, the **intent** is to hurt, embarrass, or confuse the other person, or to make a joke at their expense. This supposedly gives the first person an advantage, a "feather in his cap," or a more "honored" place with coworkers, which is the purpose of the whole activity. However, there are many dangers: from permanently hurting an important relationship, to taking on someone who is crueler than you, or perhaps going too far and giving yourself a black mark with all the by-standers. If you win, the win is often hollow.

"RIGHTEOUS INDIGNATION" -- GREAT STUFF

What a powerful position to use to evaluate – and respond to – the world around us. From this position, we can insist our way is the best and only way…because it is. No matter what topic we pick, we are right, and we deserve to be slightly obnoxious about it. There are many situations in which people adopt this stance, believing they truly know more than anyone else: politics, religion, teaching, and sometimes even in the sciences.

As Dr. Phil might say, "How's that working for you?" A haughty position surely drives others away or creates much defensiveness, or both. Of course, righteous indignation does sort of protect me, by helping me affirm I am right. But, a better stance for me – and for my relationships – is to concede the possibility I could be wrong . . . I am probably wrong a lot . . . and I likely have made unnecessary, hurtful comments to others. A bit of *humble pie* may be beneficial as I seek good interactions with others from here on out, and genuine respect for the things I really do know.

TRUE FRIENDS ARE RARE

There seems to be a trend for us to assume having a friend is easy and anyone can have many, many friends. The truth is, good friends do not "happen" often. One estimate I saw, years ago, cautioned that the average person has between two and four good friends *in a lifetime*. The rest of our "friends" are really acquaintances. When I talk with clients, they often believe there is something wrong with them, because they do not have a full quota of friends, maybe 5, or 10, or just 3 – at any one time. It helps to realize these numbers are unrealistic, so these expectations can be adjusted and allow people to be appreciative of the few, good friends they have.

Most of us are familiar with the saying, "To have a friend, you must be a friend." This is good advice, because it puts the "control" back in our hands, urging each of us to be kind, stay in touch, be available, don't stay upset over small stuff ("And it's all small stuff"). As we practice *being* a good friend, we are more likely to *find* a good friend.

FRIENDS ARE THE FAMILY WE CHOOSE

I have heard many of my clients say they have difficulty relating to their families, even difficulty fitting in, trusting, or feeling comfortable when around them. A bigger frustration is that their families do not give and receive support and encouragement, as they hoped. Clients and others have said they would never choose some of their family members as friends if they had a choice. Well, there is a choice - to choose friends to be "family members." Instead of feeling sorry for ourselves – our families are distant, cold, opinionated, or have an agenda – we can find people to invite in, to be "part of our family." Having choices contributes greatly to confidence in many areas, but I believe *this* choice is near the top of the list.

"IF I WERE YOU, I KNOW EXACTLY WHAT I WOULD DO"

It's easy to know how we would handle a situation or problem, when the problem belongs to someone else! We may be free with our advice about *how* they should handle it. In reality, we do *not* know. We do not know the history of this problem, and we do not know all the surrounding issues. We are not aware of the other problems this person may be handling at the same time, or their confidence level. In fairness, we cannot be sure how all those pieces would affect *us*, so we **do not know** the right response—for them or for us.

The following one-liners regarding perspectives of others require no explanation:

OTHERS ARE INFLUENCED MORE BY YOUR ACTIONS, THAN BY YOUR OPINIONS
Like a quote by Paulo Coelho

WE WOULD ALL DO WELL TO LISTEN MORE AND TALK LESS
Diogenes

HE WHO TALKS THE MOST USUALLY HAS THE LEAST TO SAY
Matthew Prior

Chapter 4

PERSPECTIVES ABOUT FAMILIES

WE ARE OFTEN NICER TO OUR FRIENDS THAN TO OUR OWN FAMILY

This idea fits well with the notion of "taking for granted," which explains what many of us seem to do with our families. We often forget to give them the usual and customary level of respect or appreciation, time or attention, credit or thanks. A big part of this hinges on how we expect them to know how we think and feel, without actually having to say the words. "They know I appreciate what they do" or "He kind of lets me know with some of his actions," really? This is illustrated in a bad joke from years ago in which a woman said to her husband, "You never tell me you love me anymore," to which he responded, "I told you once; if I change my mind, I'll let you know." One reason we do not work harder with family is we assume they will hang around, no matter what we say, do/don't do, or how we look; on the other hand, we know if we are not respectful in all these ways to friends, they will likely move on.

There was a popular movement several years ago about "random acts of kindness." It focused on doing nice things for strangers, and it made somewhat of a hit. Well, what about doing the same for our families: what about random kindness, for no special reason, to show appreciation? Doing this with strangers, even for a short time, really made people aware of doing something nice. Let's revive "acts of kindness" for strangers and for family.

LOVE INVOLVES MANY PIECES -- RESPECT, APPRECIATION, ENJOYING A PERSON, FORGIVENESS, COMMUNICATION, AND A DECISION TO SUPPORT THEM

Defining *love* is nearly impossible, and each person who tries has a different idea about what *love* is. Here is a definition from my experience: I suggest love requires each of the characteristics above. **Respect** is accepting the other person as they are, without trying to change them. It also involves trust and avoiding needless criticism and put-downs. (By the way, constructive criticism is ok, and can be vital to the relationship.) **Appreciation** refers to giving positive feedback, telling the person what you value about them, showing you honor who they are, and maybe hugging them affectionately. **Enjoying them** has to do with noticing them, being clear you are glad they're there, and sharing, laughing, and smiling together. **Forgiveness** means letting go of old hurts, releasing the other person as responsible for those hurts, and agreeing to move forward with hope. **Communication** means talking and listening, so feelings get addressed and problems get resolved; workable compromises are part of this. The **decision** involves making a commitment that endures through the hard times and agreeing to nurture and encourage the other person, although our natural response might be negative or critical. If this sounds like WORK, then I have portrayed my idea of *love* accurately. So, roll up your sleeves!

Since each of these parts is important, when any part is missing from the relationship, there is automatically a weakening of the connection. If more pieces stop working, both people feel the loss. Some couples try to ignore the negative changes, but eventually the weakening is obvious to them (and to others). Some people try to maintain the appearance of a marriage, but they have become more like convenient roommates. This is a sad situation for both, unless they are able to admit the problem and seek help, benefitting the couple as well as their families and their friends.

IS IT OK TO STOP WORKING AT 5:00?

Years ago, in a college chemistry lab, I learned an important psychological tip. As the clock approached 5:00, I commented to the instructor I was glad I could soon quit working and go home. He responded, "Oh?" My curiosity was up, so I asked what he meant. He wondered if I did not work around my family, if I made no effort with the people I claimed to care about the most? Clearly, his comment stuck with me, and since then I have learned more about the *work* it takes to make family relationships prosper. Part of love involves the nurturing of family members. And that means *work*.

IN WORKABLE MARRIAGES, BOTH PEOPLE KNOW IT'S NOT 50-50

Remember the fairy tales we heard as children which always ended with "...And they lived happily ever after?" Well, this image implies no work is needed to make a relationship succeed on and on; but, as most of us know, this is not true. A good relationship definitely requires work, even after years of success. Still, this work can take on a negative aspect, as many of us "keep score" and believe the work is not evenly shared. Often, the work we do seems - at the moment at least - greater than the benefit we get back: more like 60-40. How unfair!

Wait, there is another way to see this: by taking a broader perspective, the "unfairness" evens out. How do we do this? By realizing there are times in any marriage when - if we are honest - either person may give only 40% and then get back 60%. The idea of a 50-50 relationship is misleading, and often causes people to set unreasonable expectations for their partner. When we think in terms of 60-40, there is a better likelihood we can avoid some of those impossible expectations, and both people will be more satisfied with the outcome.

½ PERSON + ½ PERSON = 1 GOOD MARRIAGE?

This equation appears to be simple, accurate math. In reality it cannot work. Often, young people - and sometimes older people, too - mistakenly search for their "other half" or "a person to complete me." This means they are only half a person and need someone to make them *feel whole*. Marriage based on this idea does not fare well, because each person is *needy* and dependent on their new, other half. What does work is new math: one whole person getting together with another whole person, makes one whole relationship: 1 + 1 = 1. This kind of math can work.

COMPROMISE REQUIRES RESPECT

Couples who struggle to make decisions together are often urged to compromise. This means finding a solution which contains a some of what each person wants or finding a solution half-way between their two different ideas. Or, another option is for one person gets what they want first, and then the other person gets what they wished later. This kind of compromise may require a bit of creativity to find a suitable answer for both parties. It also requires each person to be willing to "give a little," since neither one gets all they want.

While it sounds simple and straightforward, there is another necessary, often-overlooked ingredient for compromise to occur - **respect.** If either person does not respect the other person, or that person's position, then they may stubbornly hold on to their solution and refuse to meet half-way. After all, "if my solution makes sense and yours does not, why would I respect it or meet you half-way?" Only by truly respecting each other are both people able to **accept** the other person's position. This acceptance is required, *even when they do not agree with, do not like, or do not understand the other person's point of view.* This is the essence of respect - which ultimately allows for a workable compromise.

AGREE TO DISAGREE

In my experience with clients, couples often fight and argue with no resolution, because they get stuck on the idea of who is right. Each insists on their own viewpoint. Since they are two different people with different backgrounds, they are likely to see many things differently. Rather than get stuck on this point, and never be able to achieve solutions, my recommendation is to **agree to disagree**. This is a valuable position, and can do wonders to make a relationship work. The people involved can focus on finding a workable resolution suitable to both, instead of arguing on and on about who is right.

This seemingly simple idea can be difficult to follow, if one person in the relationship is more dominant. I had a couple where the man was a lawyer and the wife was a housewife. He often overwhelmed her with his explanations and his emphasis, and her ideas had little chance of survival. With couple's therapy, they were able to make great strides in communication, when before she had always "caved in" and suffered in silence.

FINDING OUT WHO IS AT FAULT IS NOT USEFUL

In couple's therapy, blame is often the first direction each person takes. By saying, essentially, "I am blameless, and the whole problem is with the other person," the speaker does not offer to participate in improving the relationship. Yet, for growth to occur, it is essential for each person to accept his/her own responsibility for the problems and the solutions in the relationship. Then, therapy can focus fairly on the relationship, not one individual who is to blame. From this perspective, therapy can look at various ways to improve the relationship, such as communication, respect for both people, compromise and honoring what each one wants, and increased positive interactions. Each of these ideas, without fault-finding, can make a big difference in how the relationship feels and how the couple functions together.

DO YOU WANT TO BE RIGHT ...OR IN A RELATIONSHIP?
Kelly Bryson

This one-liner fits well with the previous ones and has to do with respect - and with whose opinion counts. I have met many people who work hard to let others know how much they "know." These individuals usually have difficulty allowing anyone else to have a legitimate opinion. Obviously, this can be a major hardship on a relationship, and it raises the question of which is more important - the relationship or being right? Hopefully, they can recognize they are *in* the relationship because they value the other person - and that person's views. From this perspective, they can be urged to let go of the need to be right. With more urging, maybe they can agree to disagree and even honor the ideas of the other person.

BE SURE YOU SAY SOMETHING NICE

There is another old story about a shy, pre-teen boy had just completed finishing school. There was a dance to show off everyone's new skills. His mother was with him, and when everyone else was dancing, she urged him to do the same. He reluctantly went on

59

the dance floor and asked the only girl left to dance. After just a moment of dancing, the girl ran from the room; she was crying hard. His mother rushed over to see what happened. He explained, "I was trying to remember what I was taught." "Yes, yes," said his mother, "then what?" "I tried to think of something nice to say." "Yes, yes, and then what?" asked the mother. "Well, I told her for a fat girl she didn't sweat much." Hopefully, we have the wisdom to find "nicer" things to praise than this.

TRY TO "CATCH YOUR KIDS BEING GOOD."

We are familiar with the idea of catching children when they are "being bad." To make an effort to be more positive with our children, it can be fun to "catch them being good." This helps us focus on their cooperation, not their selfishness, and on their successes, instead of their failures. In turn, this idea allows us to say nice things to them (not just complain). The next time they are playing well with someone, making an effort to clean their room, carrying dishes to the kitchen sink, or picking up their shoes, we can "catch them" and thank them for doing good. This way, we can shift the feel of our interactions with our children. (By the way, I hope we always view our children as "being good," so this goal is actually about catching them *doing* good.)

THINKING POSITIVES IS GOOD, SAYING THEM IS BETTER

Many families and couples have appreciation for what others in the family do - in their heads. Unfortunately, "positive feedback" may never get spoken, even though it is considered, but just gets taken for granted: "They know I appreciate that," "They can tell by my actions," "It's embarrassing to have to say the words," "They just know." Since the "appreciation" one feels is never actually said, the other person (or people) will never find out. This is as true between adults as it is between adults and children. Instead, please let others know your appreciation; speak up and state what you like. Other family communications are likely to improve as well.

APOLOGIES ARE VALUABLE, BUT . . .

Despite the seemingly obvious value of apologies, they can be quite tricky; because of this, apologies often do not work. This seems to happen because people are reluctant to give a really good apology and tend to give a half, flimsy, or conditional apology. Saying we're sorry really loses power and effectiveness, when the wording includes any of these: "**If** I hurt you . . .," "**In case** I did something wrong . . .," "If I **maybe** . . .," "I'm sorry **you** *took* **it** . . .," or "I'm sorry **you heard** . . ." Each of these puts blame on the other person, as if I did not do anything wrong. These messages clearly say they *interpreted* my (rude, mean) comment incorrectly. Similarly, telling the other person they are "over-reacting" will undoubtedly ruin any apology. Thus, these are not apologies at all, but **veiled blame.**

Another common practice that ruins apologies is attaching an excuse or explanation. "I am sorry I am late for the meeting again, but that same train was stopped on the tracks again." By using an excuse, I really minimize any responsibility for my action. In the example I just used, there is no indication I will attempt to fix the problem, like by leaving home earlier. With family members, it seems we often excuse away our behavior and still call it an apology.

A different approach is to be genuine with the apology, and express sorrow for any hurt I caused. Most of the time, this can be simple and straight-forward: "I am really sorry I forgot your birthday." At other times, some tact may be helpful, especially when I am not sorry for what I said or did. There are times when I meant what I said or did, but I did not intend for that to hurt the other person. At those times, I may be able to practice tact, by carefully apologizing not for what I did, but only for the hurt I caused. For example, "I am sorry my opinion about your new dress upset you." You see, I did not apologize for my negative opinion, just the hurt. Or, another example, "I am sorry my view of your mother is so different than yours, and my view bothers you so much." Again, I am not apologizing for my view being somehow wrong, only for it being problematic. So, if my deeds seem honorable and reasonable to me, I can apologize only for the *hurt* they caused, and *not* for the actions. I believe this allows me to be more honest

WATCH YOUR Ps and Ds
Thibaut and Kelley

A number of years ago, a study looked closely at the *pleasing (Ps)* and *displeasing (Ds)* things happening within marriages. A large number of couples were instructed to tally the *Ps* and *Ds* they received from their spouse for two weeks, then return to finish the study. Before turning in their tally sheets, each person rated the quality of their relationship over the last two-week period. The results showed when the ratio of *Ps* and *Ds* averaged 1:1 (maybe 30 P's and 32 Ds during the two weeks), the couples rated their relationship for those weeks as "poor." When the ratio averaged 2:1, the quality rating was "so-so." When the ratio was 3:1, the overall rating was reported as "good." Conclusion: couples feel better about their marriage when there are significantly more pleasing actions that displeasing ones. So, to improve any relationship, increase the *Ps* and decrease the *Ds*.

Some other interesting observations came from this research. When one person in the couple guessed and thought they knew what their partner liked, ie, what was a *P*, they were often wrong and so they "missed" (no P). In addition, participants often had no idea if what they had given was a *P* or *D*, because there was *no feedback from their partner*. Another observation: participants often did well with a different partner (someone they did not know): seemingly, they did have the ability to know and dispense Ps and Ds. Finally, men and women were different - big surprise - and often "missed" each other, because *they gave what they liked*, and this was not a *P* for their opposite-sexed partner.

An important caution came out of the study: "Excuses do not change the *Ds*." Excuses—which many of us are so good at— usually become *more Ds*, which we then must balance with *more Ps*. Eliminating excuses and minimizing some Ds (we can never fully eliminate them), can be a simple and helpful way to improve a relationship.

WARM FUZZIES ARE BEST, BUT COLD PRICKLIES ARE BETTER THAN NOTHING
Claude Steiner

In any relationship, what gets exchanged with the other person affects each person and the relationship. One popular theory in psychology identifies positive responses between people and calls these *warm fuzzies*. Because these warm fuzzies are positive, people are willing to work for them, to accumulate more. According to the theory, some interactions between people result in **nothing** being shared; this nothing is not worth working for, so people generally are not interested in accumulating more *nothing*. The theory goes further and identifies *cold pricklies*, which are worth something, and people are willing to work some to get them. Therefore, a *cold prickly* is better than nothing at all. So, what are these things? An example of a warm fuzzy could be a compliment, a raise, or a "thank you." An example of a cold prickly could be a punch on the shoulder, teasing, or a put down. And, an example of nothing might involve being ignored. As you can see, a cold prickly is negative, but still something. It can help us understand each other by looking closely at interactions – warm fuzzies, cold pricklies, or nothing; it does make a difference.

Maybe you can help me out with a nagging question: years ago another therapist I worked with told me I was the first person he ever met who could give *warm pricklies* and *cold fuzzies*. I never could figure out what he was saying, and he would never explain. Do you suppose he was giving me a cold prickly, in the form of a back-handed criticism?

I KNOW JUST HOW YOU FEEL

This statement always reminds me of a cartoon drawing with an overweight male doctor (picture a large stomach) and a very pregnant woman, both standing in profile and looking like mirror images. The caption had the doctor saying, "I know just how you feel." But, wait. No, he doesn't. In fact, none of us can ever know how someone else feels. Even when we think our situations are the same, there are differences in our backgrounds, support systems, and previous experiences which may be huge. We need to stop thinking we know how someone else feels. Instead, try telling them, "I don't know how you feel. I can only try to understand."

Some time ago, I consulted with Compassionate Friends, which is a support group for parents who have lost a child. One of the frustrations I heard many times was this statement. People who had lost a parent, or a friend, or a cat tried to express their understanding by saying, "I know just . . ." From the feedback I heard, this was never reassuring and never seemed accurate. So, I recommend we all try another way to express our sympathy.

CHILDREN ARE MORE LIKELY TO FEEL VALUED AND PROTECTED WHEN PARENTS CARE ENOUGH TO SAY NO
Like a quote by William Sears

I think parenting is a very hard job - and it comes with no training manual. One hard part of this is being able to say "No." I believe it is helpful to know our children need us to say "No;" this assures them we are looking out for their welfare and we want to avoid possible harm for them. Our children may not appreciate it at the time, although they may in the future. I believe if we *never* say "No," it tells them we don't care.

A friend shared with me that, when his daughter was in college at about age 22, she questioned him about a party he would not let her attend in high school. At first, he did not know what she meant, so she reminded him: she was 15, it was after a school play, no parents were to be there, and a keg was planned. My friend remembered then, and felt sure of his decision from seven years earlier. But, his daughter said, "That is the only thing I will never forgive you for." He was devastated for several days, until he realized what she said: this was the *only* thing she will never forgive. He was greatly relieved. Even though his daughter was still upset about that "NO," he was convinced he did the right thing and did protect her. I hope he had other memories of saying "NO," and this time getting a positive response from his daughter. Nevertheless, saying "No" is one of the most difficult – and most important – parts of parenting.

OFFER ONLY BRIEF ANSWERS TO CHILDREN'S QUESTIONS

When young children ask questions, we often think we can give them the full story, because we know exactly what they are asking and what they need to know. But, if we are wrong, we may offer too much information or information they do not really want. We are better off giving a brief answer, seeing if they have another question, and – if they do – answer that one briefly, too. In the process, we may or may not discover the direction they are headed with their questions. Consider this: an eight-year-old boy asked his father where he came from. His father, thinking this was the time for "the birds and the bees" talk, gave the youngster an hour-long lecture on sex, babies, and birth. At the end, the father asked, "Did that answer your question, son?" To which, the boy replied, "Billy said he was from Chicago. I just wondered where I was from."

CHILDREN OFTEN VENT THEIR ANGER AT THE "SAFE" PARENT

Many parents have asked me why their children are angry with them, when clearly the other parent is the cause of the child's frustration. This happens often in divorces, when the more caring and available parent seems to catch all the flack. I believe there is a reason why the caring parent catches more grief: children know to be careful around the parent who walked away, for fear that parent will walk away from them, too. Instead of showing anger with that parent, the child directs feelings toward the parent who is safe - the one who is not likely to react badly or leave. Certainly, this makes sense and may show our children's wisdom. While it may not seem very fair at the time, the child is actually trusting and complimenting the parent who is caring, always there, and safe.

THE BEST THING A FATHER CAN DO FOR HIS CHILDREN IS TO LOVE THEIR MOTHER
Elaine Dalton

We put so much emphasis on how fathers need to spend time with their children, how they need to be there at key times in the child's life. Many stress how the father needs to listen and support, not criticize. Surely, those things are important; but, let's not forget that simply loving the child's mother and demonstrating that *around* the child is a really important message, too.

THE FRONTAL CORTEX OF YOUNG PEOPLE IS NOT DEVELOPED — SO DON'T EXPECT RATIONAL DECISIONS

My wife often reminds our three children (late teen/early twenties) she wants to help them make big decisions, because they are not yet "rational." She interferes very little with their lives, but does inject reason when they seem off target. I believe this is a good practice - at least until their brains develop fully. (That's around 35 years old, isn't it?)

NEVER LOAN MONEY TO A RELATIVE -- GIFT IT
Dave Ramsey

This was valuable advice given to me years ago by a very wise friend. When we loan something, we expect eventually, or sooner,

65

to get it back. Often with family members, getting things back falls apart, seemingly because "we're all family here." Whether it is money, tools, a used crib, or a set of china, the loaner often seems to experience much anxiety, due to waiting and hoping. Also, the loaner may stress about finding the right time to ask for a return. And then, there is the strain of being polite at family functions where the tension may run high, anyway. Anger or resentment can build up, and take a toll on the loaner. To avoid this stress and make this much more pleasant, the loaner can consider either giving the money (or other item) as a gift . . . or say "No."

SECRETS ARE CHARACTERISTIC OF DYSFUNCTIONAL FAMILIES
Donna LaMar

It is helpful to me, in my work with families, to realize keeping secrets is a normal and even required part of how dysfunctional families operate. In these families, for me to get important information can be difficult, because they have a pact to *not* talk about problems. To some extent, all families have this rule or a similar one: "We don't air our dirty linen in public." Unfortunately, this can put much stress on children who may be suffering and struggling in the family, but are not allowed to talk about it. They can be confused about telling anyone, including teachers, pediatricians, therapists...or even the police. As professionals who work with children understand this rule, they can be more successful exploring issues with these children, and, of course, more helpful.

CHAPTER 5

PERSPECTIVES ABOUT LIFE

SEEING LIFE IN DIFFERENT WAYS IS NORMAL AND ENRICHING

There is a theory that if all humans saw everything the same way, life would be dull. For good or bad, we do not see the world exactly alike, but we have quite different perspectives of the world and how the world functions. This fact makes for both excitement and struggles, as we share life with others. This fact does encourage us to think more broadly, not just from our own preconceived perspective, or maybe our own comfort zone. It is ok and quite beneficial to honor differences in our world views.

IN LIFE, STRUGGLING IS NATURAL, BUT SUFFERING IS OPTIONAL
Like a quote by Haruke Murakami

There seems to be a tendency for people believe what happens around them is the direct cause of their suffering, emotional pain, and unhappiness. The truth is, how we look at life around us is the cause of such feelings. The idea that our existence involves struggle seems perfectly normal. But to say those struggles automatically cause us to suffer seems worth questioning, since this idea does not fit everyone's experience. There are people who are handicapped or severely limited, but have amazing attitudes and accomplish amazing things. What makes *suffering optional* is how each of us handles and thinks about what we find right in front of our noses. This **perspective** – not the situation over which we struggle – determines our reactions and feelings.

Mahatma Gandhi and the Dalai Lama apparently know and fully tap into this principle. Every time I have seen videos of them, they are positive, forgiving, and <u>not</u> suffering, despite many struggles. It is hard to imagine either of them becoming outwardly upset, even by a difficult situation. It appears their perspective allows them to remain at peace, and avoid suffering.

It is important to note an exception to this – a startle response, from a sudden noise or unexpected surprise. This will set off automatic, protective responses in all of us, often referred to as fight-flight. These are perfectly normal, and we have little control over them. However, how long those startle responses continue depends on our mental reaction, ie, how long we hold on to or dwell on negative thoughts.

LIFE IS 10% WHAT HAPPENS TO YOU AND 90% WHAT YOU DO WITH IT
Charles Swindell

A tendency in our society is to blame others for our unhappiness, and we especially blame our parents. This eliminates our responsibility, giving a convenient excuse to be "stuck." But, as adults, we are in charge of our lives, and how we cope is up to us; we need to take our power back. We can get ourselves *unstuck* when we see we have power and when we understand we have a "say" in our lives today. Even a sail boat is not simply at the mercy of the wind, because a skillful sailor can move in any direction – even into the wind – by tacking. We have all heard the saying, "If life gives you lemons, make lemonade;" this really embodies the spirit of *doing the best I can with any situation.*

Many people believe "things happen for a reason" and there is no such thing as "coincidence." When we start to think this way, we are more likely to see an event as an *opportunity*, not a hindrance, and look for options which work for us. We might find ourselves being creative as we address difficult situations, you know, "thinking outside the box."

What does this look like in everyday situations? If you get stuck in traffic, and cannot move at all, consider turning on the radio, laying your seat back, removing your shoes, and resting. Another example: I was to testify in court recently, but discovered I had a long wait before being called. I do not like to waste time, so I went into the situation prepared. I got out a pad of paper and wrote several pages of this book. I stayed calm and got some valuable work done. If in your life, you find yourself in another argument with your partner, you can choose to stop an unproductive habit and take a "time out." This allows both of you to cool off, so you can talk more constructively later. If your partner objects to "time out," use the infallible statement: "Diarrhea . . . I really have to go." It is your choice to stand there and have another hurtful, pointless exchange or try something new. Remember, what I do with what I am given determines 90% of the outcome. How you "take care of it" is your choice. Make it a good one!

IF YOU INSIST ON FIGHTING REALITY, YOU WILL LOSE.

This may seem obvious, but many people seem to fight reality without realizing what they are doing. "If the weather is not good on my birthday, it will kill me." "It is terrible our government is so full of politics." "I can't believe everyone does not agree with me about this." Seriously, reality is not going to cooperate with any of these statements, so the result will definitely be a losing situation. "I know I did not study much for this test, but I had better make an 'A' or I'm in big trouble." "How are you supposed to exercise when it makes you sweat so much?" And a big one: "Life should be different than it is . . . it should be my way all the time." These are sure ways to lose.

This does not mean we should give up trying to change things around us. In some situations, we can, and many of us will. Of course, it helps to be wise about what we take on to change. (Sounds like the Serenity Prayer, doesn't it?) And, continuing to fight about a reality that consistently has not changed, despite many attempts, is silly; I would be best off to stop challenging this "immovable object."

JUDGMENT vs DISCERNMENT

Years ago, I thought these two words were interchangeable. Then, a little research showed me there is a huge difference. Both involve making a decision about what is good or bad, but judgment means criticizing, not just the event or decision, but also the person responsible, as being "bad." In contrast, discernment means deciding if a situation or a person's behavior(s) is "bad" as it applies to *me*; there is no criticism of the person involved. I believe discernment is necessary for emotionally healthful living, but judgment is hurtful to others, as well as to me.

DO YOU LIVE TO WORK OR WORK TO LIVE?
Jody Michael

The answer to this simple question can have a large effect on one's life, and represents an important perspective toward life. *People who live to work* make their job or career their focus. Other parts of their life get less attention. Those "other parts" might be a partner, family, friends, health, fun, or spirituality. On the other hand, *people who work to live* use their job as one source of what they value in life, and they use the money they earn to *enjoy* the "other parts" (see list, above). I once heard a minister say he had talked to many people on their death bed, and they expressed many regrets – but he never heard anyone who wished they had spent more time at work. Imagine that.

TAKE A BREAK—IT HELPS EVERYTHING

Hard work is esteemed in our society and reflected in sayings we use: "hard work is next to Godliness" and "there is no rest for the weary." To the contrary, I recommend taking breaks - to be rejuvenated, to get a new perspective on a problem, and to improve your learning potential. Years ago, a study was done with college students, in which two groups studied for three hours. One group studied straight through and the other group took ten-minute breaks every hour. As you might guess, the group taking breaks performed better on the final evaluation than the straight-though group. In everyday life, a break can be just as helpful, to restore alertness, concentration, and energy, while lowering anxiety and tension.

When I was a teenager, my brother and I were repairing his car. We were nearly done, with only one bolt to put back. We both knew where it went, and we both tried to get it to go in - but it would not. Frustrated, we took a break, got a drink (of water), talked with our parents, and then approached the bolt again. As you might guess, it went in easily. It did not change, we did, and the change in us made quite a difference.

THE LONGEST JOURNEY BEGINS WITH THE FIRST STEP
Confucius

"I can't do it, it's too big." "Where do I start, I have no idea." "I don't know how to get there from here." "What if I get lost?" "A college degree at my age? That would take forever." Often we agonize over new problems, because our perspective makes them seem impossible to accomplish. It is easier to delay or give up, when we look at the whole task and get overwhelmed. It helps to know we do not need to have all the answers at the beginning; we only need to know where to start. Generally, we can figure out or discover the rest, later. We benefit by taking that first step. After all, this creates momentum, clarifies the journey, and opens up options we could not see before we started. Go ahead, take that first step!

"CRAZY BEHAVIOR" CAN BE NORMAL.

This may sound impossible, but I would like for you to consider this possibility for a moment:

> Crazy behavior in a normal situation is crazy (#1); normal behavior in a crazy situation is also crazy (#2); but, crazy behavior in a crazy situation is normal (#3).

Imagine people in a theater. If one person in the theater starts running around frantically, speaking loudly, insisting "Do you see the IRS agents up there? They are here to steal my mind. Help me, help me." Clearly, this is odd behavior for an otherwise common situation (an example for #1), and I would refer to this as **crazy**. Now, consider another person in the movie theater staying in their seat and yawning after another person yelled "Fire!" This behavior would seem inappropriate for this particular situation, and I call this **crazy**, too. Now for the third example: if, in the same theater, someone was crying, yelling, and pushing to get out, after hearing

"Fire!" their behavior would easily be considered appropriate for this unusual (crazy) situation. I would call this **normal behavior.**

I have had many clients who thought their feelings and/or behavior were crazy, but they had forgotten they were clearly in "crazy" situations. Their irritability, poor concentration, frequent crying, or headaches could all be in response to unusual and difficult circumstances, like a pending divorce, news someone close to them has cancer, the "empty nest," or talk of big layoffs at work. These situations are stressful, unexpected, and often several together, or in other words - crazy. Why would we not act in strange ways in such situations? I urge clients to go easy on themselves when this occurs. One common crazy situation is grief; people often **feel crazy** as they try to cope with the loss of a special person, plus all the other changes that occur simultaneously. But, their experience is definitely normal.

GRIEF IS OFTEN GREATLY MISUNDERSTOOD

The norm in our society about grieving is "It is ok to grieve for two weeks, but then you should get your act together." Two weeks – really? Most professionals lean toward two *years* for an **uncomplicated bereavement.** Then, if the loss is complex, it may take considerably longer to work through. Such **complicated grief** may result from a suicide, the death of a child, or from within a dysfunctional relationship. Promising Dad, on his death bed, "I will not put Mom in a nursing home," can cause serious, complicated grief, too.

I believe grieving people often are not given **permission to grieve** fully. Since their sorrow makes others uncomfortable, anyone grieving may be instructed to get over it quickly, but they cannot.

This is partly because grieving involves many different feelings, from sadness to anger, to fear, to guilt. And to complicate recovery further, a previous loss can **piggyback** on a current loss, making for a more confusing, and lengthy grief. Finally, if the person grieving was ever encouraged to **stuff their feelings**, especially about past losses, these emotions could easily show up during this current grief - whether the losses are related or not.

GRIEF IS SOMETHING TO WORK THROUGH, NOT HEAL OR FIX

Grief is **normal** - an automatic, human response to loss. There is *no need to heal it*, because it is not a sickness. There is also *no need to fix it*, since nothing is broken. It can be valuable to think of grief work – and it is work – as doing what it takes to *work through the grief*. This involves primarily dealing with the many feelings, so the person can eventually put those feelings behind him/her. The goal is *not* to forget the person who died, nor is the goal to never feel sadness again. The goal is to move on with life - which the person(s) who died would probably want, anyway.

What does it mean to **work though grief**? I warn my clients it is similar to going through a swamp. It is not pleasant, there is no way around, and you are likely to get stuck several times. You probably will be bothered by nasty bugs and critters (doubt, criticism, and red eyes). To get to the other side, you must go straight through. Allow the feelings, honor them, and work through them (with writing, talking, expressing, etc.). The final goal is to find a way to live without the other person, and then begin to create a new life experience.

GEOGRAPHIC CURES DON'T WORK

"If only I could live in New York, where all the excitement and opportunities are. Then, I would be happy." "If only I could get out of the crowded city, with its continual rat race, then I could relax and have time for hobbies." We have all heard these wish-filled statements, but there is an inherent flaw in them, ie, **Wherever I go, I have to take me with**. Any move I make does *not* automatically change *my* habits, hurtful beliefs, impossible expectations, family conditioning, or my fears. All those influential anchors go with me, and therefore life in any new location goes on pretty much as it did before I moved. We can only wish it were so simple.

"THE HURRIER I GO, THE BEHINDER I GET"
Old Pennsylvania Dutch saying

The wisdom of this one-liner apparently has been known for a long time, thanks to the Pennsylvania Dutch. We all have been in a big hurry sometime, and because of that we started making mistakes. As we try to catch up by moving faster, hoping to get things done quickly and get back on schedule, we make more mistakes. It seems it happens to all of us, and someone created this saying to capture this truth. It also provides a good reminder we would all benefit from slowing down.

IT'S HARD TO NOTICE THE ABSENCE OF SOMETHING

This saying helps to bring to awareness something that is easily overlooked. When we or others make changes in behavior, the goal is often to stop annoying others or ourselves (or stop harming someone). When we are successful in stopping an upsetting act - for example, leaving shoes by the front door - the other person may not notice; in fact, we may stop noticing, too. Or, let's say we make an effort to stop using "Um" before every sentence. If we succeed, others will not necessarily notice. It can be the same way with a rattling cough, leaving coffee cups on the living room table, interrupting, being late, leaving the toilet seat up, or a whole host of annoying behaviors. So, if you are hoping for appreciation each time **you don't do** something, it may not happen; the other person may never notice what does not happen.

A CHAIN ALWAYS BREAKS AT ITS WEAKEST LINK

In a literal sense, this is easy to see and accept. But, it is harder to apply to our day-to-day functioning. I believe applying it means we are most affected by stress, tension, fatigue, and grief at the physical or emotional place where we are weakest. If someone has long-standing back problems, job stress is likely to make it worse. The stress may not show up anywhere else, since "back" is the weakest link. Chronic sleep deprivation might "show up" as an emotional weak spot, like ones tendency to be irritable or easily angered. Tension from finances could cause stomach upset, which may have been learned - as a weak spot - from a father who used Maalox daily. This is why recovering alcoholics often return to drinking - it is their weakest point when stress hits.

YESTERDAY WENT PRETTY WELL -- ALL BY ITSELF

Many of us seem to attribute success and good times to nebulous sources, rather than to ourselves. In the statement above, "yesterday" seems to get the credit for the day going well, completely on its own. In a similar way, we often give credit for our successes or "good days" to "things" (going well), "good luck," "sheer chance," "them," or "being in the right place at the right time." I believe this is *misdirected credit*; the emphasis would be best put on the genuine probability **I created** my own "good day." We unknowingly give away the credit for many achievements, by stating "yesterday" or "luck" should get the credit. No, No, No. We benefit by taking reasonable credit for successes, because this (1) increases **our self-esteem** and (2) shows us what we can **do next time** to achieve another success. I do not mean to exclude good luck or beneficial circumstances entirely, but I suggest *keeping in perspective how much each of us does to achieve success.*

Maybe an example will help. Recently, I noticed I felt very good at the end of my day. So, I intentionally looked back to understand why. I was able to list a series of successes: one client was very grateful for the weeks of support and ideas I gave her, another therapist thanked me for help with a problem that had her stuck, my wife was excited to meet me for dinner out when I asked, I stayed focused on my paperwork and finished it quickly, I took advantage of a free moment to glance through a new book. What I noticed in this list was the large number of "I's" which let me know that the good day was what I created (with a little help from others). Giving myself credit is very beneficial.

THE WORLD SHOULD BE FAIR -- RIGHT?

This is an interesting myth. It often occurs in the form of "Oh, that is not fair, and it should be." A closer look at our world shows clearly many aspects of life are not fair - period. Good people get cancer, promotions are given to the boss' relatives, the rich get richer, world-class runners fall, and teachers sometimes miss the student who started the scuffle. These are all examples of how the world is not fair. Accepting that many events are negative or unfair allows us to start letting go of this upsetting myth and its expectations, and in turn letting go of the upsetting feelings resulting from it. By the way, it helps to remember: sometimes the world *is* fair, and we *are* acknowledged for our contribution or rewarded for our hard work.

TIME HEALS ALL WOUNDS -- RIGHT?

This is another time-honored myth. From a purely physical viewpoint, an injury resulting in a gash does not heal if only given "time." This wound requires cleaning, maybe an antibacterial ointment, protection, good nutrition, and time. Emotional wounds also need more than just time; these wounds need permission to feel and process those feelings, an opportunity to vent, some degree of self-confidence, and support from others. Time helps, but again it is not the only necessary ingredient.

THINGS WILL WORK OUT IN THE END -- RIGHT?

NO. Here is yet another **myth**. This one implies **things** are somehow capable – on their own - of doing the work to resolve problematic situations. What *are* those "things" we're all counting on? What do they do? How do they solve problems? Where do they come from? The truth is things do not fix anything, rather it is *people* who resolve issues and solve problems. Things will not work out a problem, but people can. Unfortunately, if no one works on a problem, nothing will change, and it will be the same tomorrow as it is today. Dr. Seuss said it correctly, "Unless someone like you cares a whole awful lot, nothing is going to get better, it's not."

What about the problems someone makes half an effort to change? Certainly, a half-effort or just *trying* does not guarantee anything will be better in the end. In fact, "practice," according to my father, "does not make perfect, because it takes correct practice to get better at anything." Usually, people's honest efforts make a situation better; but, only *hoping* "things will work out" is a set up for disappointment.

WHEN PEOPLE LACK INFORMATION ABOUT SOMETHING, THEY USUALLY THINK THE WORST

When family members are late to arrive home, many of us worry. Then, we start to think: Did they have a wreck? Are they injured or in the hospital with a sudden illness? Generally, the truth is much simpler and blander: they stopped at the grocery store or went to visit a friend and forgot to check in. When we don't know, we tend to imagine the worst.

My favorite example of this is the people of Columbus' time. They did not know what lay far out in the ocean, so they guessed the worst possibilities - the world is flat and at the edge people will encounter monsters, fall off the edge, be swallowed up, etc., never to be seen again. Those people told Columbus he was a fool to sail out there. Today, we know a different truth - the world is not flat - and no horrendous consequence results from going there, such as falling off the edge. Are there "presumed monsters" in your life because you lack information?

FOLLOW THROUGH DOES MAKE A DIFFERENCE
Elisa Gaudet

Most people know that, in golf or tennis, follow-through in the swing affects the flight of the ball. Obviously, this can only be true because the beginning of the swing—before the ball is hit—is affected by the follow through. In the same way, our ideas about what happens after death can have an effect on the way we live each day. In my experience, even if someone has had some form of religious education, many are not sure about "after death." With older adults, this can be quite serious, perhaps resulting in or adding to depression, anxiety, or fear. This often occurs when they near the end of their lives or witness family and friends dying. Developing a clear idea about "what comes after death" can be helpful, even though none of us has any way to be sure. How clear is your idea of the "follow-through" for *your* life?

THE GOOD NEWS ABOUT PAST HURTS IS: THEY ARE OVER
Jon Connelly

Painful memories can plague people for years after the event occurs. As people recall some past event, they may become as emotional as when the event occurred; this can be especially painful and difficult to manage. Sometimes, this is referred to as a flashback (often a part of post-traumatic stress disorder) or an "ab-reaction," and it happens when our subconscious mind confuses the memory with the reality. Hypnotherapy is one powerful way to help those with these vivid memories, by focusing on clarifying *the memory is not the event*. This helps stop the confusion in the subconscious, so the memory is only seen as that, a memory, not the event reoccurring. Hypnotherapy can also help people let go of any unhealthy meaning which got attached to that memory years ago. Clearing the effects of the past in this way has appropriately been referred to as getting the "good news" to the whole mind.

WHEN YOU COME TO A ROAD BLOCK, TAKE THE DETOUR

My brother wanted to try out his new dirt bike on a brand new stretch of highway that was not open, yet. He was zipping along when he unexpectedly came upon a ten-foot break in the pavement. His bike dropped into the hole and he went over the handlebars, sliding for about forty feet on the new concrete. Hindsight is terrific, and we all know he should have heeded the warning signs and taken a detour.

In our daily lives, we see warning signs and road blocks about situations, relationships, decisions, or offers that are a little too good to be true. Sometimes, the way straight ahead seems too exciting, so we continue on, ignoring the warnings. Like my brother, we typically experience painful consequences from our failure to take a "detour" that would have saved us pain. As an example, one kind of warning sign is our own intuition; unfortunately, it speaks softly most of the time, so it is easy to ignore. There are times when we see the road block clearly, and our emotions (or unrealistic thinking) lead us to ignore the warning. An example might be starting a romantic relationship. All seems fine at first, then some history leaks that the person has been married four times, had a child that was taken away, and has been fired from six jobs in ten years. THAT is a clear detour, but many of us have ignored the warnings and pursued the relationship.

THE BEST PREDICTOR OF FUTURE BEHAVIOR ... IS PAST BEHAVIOR
Walter Mischel

While this may seem obvious, psychologists, psychiatrists, judges, teachers, college entrance decision-makers, match makers, and many others attempt to find other ways to predict who will do well, who will be honest, who will work hard, who will succeed, and who will ultimately "make it." Structured interviews, personality tests, ink blots, "trick" questions, drawings, and IQ tests have all been designed to assess a person and make predictions about the future, estimations of the present, or interpretations about the past. Some of these do a fairly good job when used by an experienced and well-informed evaluator.

And yet, the best predictor is the person's past behavior. Look there first. Someone who has held several jobs in a short time has either moved up the ladder quickly, or has failed to meet the demands of each employer. This can be important information for someone making a hiring decision *now*. Unfortunately, though this is the best "test" we have, it is not always accurate. For example, poorly-performing high school students have been known to go on the college and do extremely well. And rumor has it Einstein was kicked out of math class in the sixth grade.

LUCK? NO, THAT'S WHERE I WAS AIMING

My clients are often surprised when they achieve a goal, like laughing more or being able to relax easier. They often see this achievement as somewhat magical, thinking they do not know how the change happened. I do not question how it happened, since I know they have typically worked hard to reach their goal. So, I share this story: at an old county golf course, a new man was added to a regular threesome. When he teed off at the first hole, he made a hole-in-one; his fellow golfers were totally amazed, but he was quiet and humble. At the second tee, he again hit a hole-in-one. This time, the others were extremely impressed and praised him highly. Again, he was quiet. When they pressed him about his luck, he finally spoke up: "What do you mean luck? That's where I was aiming." Using this story, I remind people they have worked hard for their progress, and when they succeed, it is no surprise. For them, too, there is no luck involved; their success is "where they were aiming."

WE OFTEN DO NOT VALUE SOMETHING UNTIL WE LOSE IT

Yes, we often do such a good job taking for granted the things around us, we forget to appreciate or value them when we have them. We do this expecting those things will always be there when we need them. We tend to think about those enjoyable things only when they are gone. There are many movies about this, especially when "the thing" is another person. And, there are many other "things" we can take for granted for way too long: our vision, being able to drive, remembering our daily routine, having a pet, clean air and water. If these were gone, we would notice! Then we might want to express our gratitude, but it is too late.

These one-liners about perspectives on life require no explanation:

RANDOM ACTS OF KINDNESS BENEFIT EVERYONE
Like a quote by Martin Kornfeld

IF IT AINT BROKE, DON'T FIX IT.

Chapter 6

FEELINGS

FEELINGS ARE NOT GOOD OR BAD, JUST PART OF BEING HUMAN
Lawrence Kincade

In our intellectual, rational society, feelings are often considered a problem. We are typically encouraged to "think things through" or "be reasonable" about situations, "not get emotional." This places a negative value on feelings. Rather than judge them in a negative way, we may all do well to accept we are human and our feelings are part of the package. In fact, feelings often *enrich* our lives.

FEELINGS CAN BE DESIRABLE OR UNDESIRABLE, BUT THEY ARE NEVER RIGHT OR WRONG.

Many of us are quick to **judge** others' feelings - and our own, too. "That's a dumb way to feel," "You are overreacting," or "That's right, you should be upset" are often what we hear from others; all these responses are assigning right or wrong. A much better perspective is to see all feelings as neither right nor wrong. While feelings may feel bad, and we wish we did not have to deal with them, it helps to consider them as undesirable, rather than labeling them as wrong.

FEELINGS OFTEN DO NOT MAKE SENSE BECAUSE THEY ARE NOT ALWAYS RATIONAL.

Since our society often pushes for a "rational way of life," feelings may not fit. After all, feelings can be mysterious and difficult to explain, so they do not conform to *rational living*. Feelings are still a part of us, even if some people might try to eliminate them altogether. Adopting a perspective, which says it is ok if feelings are not rational, allows us to accept them as part of being human. As a simple example, we are aware our "favorite colors" may be quite difficult to explain rationally, but that does not change our color preference. Similarly, "love" does not fit rational explanation, either.

FEELINGS ARE WORTH HONORING

Another common viewpoint about feelings is to see them as a "weak" part of ourselves. When feelings seem to conflict with rational decision making or confuse the process of sorting out an important issue, these feelings might not be respected. At such times, there is a tendency to get rid of them as quickly as possible (unless the feelings happen to be "good"). If we can stop for a moment and find a way to appreciate how our feelings do enrich our lives, then we can *honor* our feelings as valuable and unique parts of all of us.

FEELINGS OFTEN OCCUR IN MULTIPLES, NOT JUST ONE AT A TIME

This is one more way feelings can be confusing and even overwhelming. Particularly with difficult situations or decisions, we often seem flooded by feelings, which makes any decision more difficult. When a family member is ill and treatment is offered with little guarantee, our several feelings definitely confuse our decision. Or even when we are stopped by a policeman, the mixed and often conflicting feelings (see next section) can add a layer of confusion about what to do. It helps to remember those same feelings - all of them – will soon be over and can enrich our lives, too.

CONTRADICTORY FEELINGS CAN OCCUR AT THE SAME TIME

This is a truly an odd aspect to feelings, ie, the idea that opposing feelings can be present simultaneously. When this occurs, it makes life extra interesting, especially when we are pushed to "make up our mind," or "keep it simple." I believe people experience this kind of contradiction often, maybe daily. An easy example might be looking at a new car: we might feel excited and happy about "that new car smell," how quietly it rides, and how comfortable it is, while at the same time feeling concerned about the first scratch, higher insurance costs, and monthly payments. A more difficult situation might be the mixed feelings surrounding a daughter getting married: happy and excited for her new life, but worried she is unprepared for this commitment. Other common situations with contradictory feelings might be selling the house you grew up in or retiring. It would seem **contradictory feelings are normal**.

FEELINGS RARELY CAUSE PROBLEMS SINCE THEY ARE BRIEF AND SPONTANEOUS

In many situations, it is common for us to have an immediate, emotional reaction. This can be positive and pleasant, or it may be uncomfortable and scary. For the most part, these situations and the feelings developing from them tend to resolve fairly quickly, resulting in a temporary, minor disturbance for us. In the case where the feelings are desirable, the situation and the feelings can be enjoyable. On the other hand, if the feelings involve intense anger or embarrassing startle, or other undesirable feelings, we may experience a "problem" or struggle as long as the feelings last. Fortunately, such everyday situations and feelings **last a rather short time typically**, according to psychological research.

However, there are times when these feelings may *not* go away or resolve quickly. This occurs especially when the feelings are *fed or reinforced with powerful, persistent, negative thoughts*. "Surprise" generally is short-lived, but well-placed thoughts can change it into anger with the person who caused the surprise, and then more thoughts can build that feeling into a major, long-term resentment. Clearly, allowing such feelings to quickly run their course may prevent any "problem" from developing, but adding negative thoughts will cause the feeling to grow.

FEELINGS THAT ARE FED CAN GO ON, AND EVEN GROW

As just described above, the normal course for feelings is to last a short time and resolve, to some extent on their own. But, we are capable of taking any situation/feeling and causing it to get bigger, by thoughts which "grow" the original feeling. Oddly, we may even create this response without really understanding what we are doing, and eventually we are likely to blame the emotion as the "problem." So, if this is not the normal flow of feelings, how do we create big emotional responses?

It is actually quite simple to do: by energetically and continually *feeding, supporting, and re-fueling* a regular feeling, such as sadness or frustration. The result is a really big emotion. Then, if we continue to feed the emotion over time, it will continue, too. This process can keep any feeling alive and well for long periods of time, and this is what often happens with us - even when we do not realize. The Hatfields and McCoys are famous for having maintained an on-going resentment lasting for generations, a resentment fed by generation after generation with "good justifications." On a more personal level, many of us hang on for weeks or months to our own resentments, as well as our hurts, sadness, or fears. We do this by reviewing the past event, reminding ourselves of our "reasons" for continuing to feel those feelings, and then reinforcing the legitimacy of our feeling right now. Emphasizing how unfair it was, as well as how **awful, or terrible, or unacceptable, or intolerable** it was feeds each feeling. Doing this gives the feeling a fresh squirt of energy, and keeps it pumped up and alive for months and years.

OVERREACTING EMOTIONALLY? -- MAYBE NOT

When we find ourselves reacting with considerable emotion to a situation, we - and others around us - think our reaction is excessive. We can be quick to criticize ourselves, and others may criticize us too, with comments like "hysterical" or "get a grip." In these situations, "just stopping" may be difficult. Instead, we may benefit from considering **all the contributors** to our reaction, ie, realizing just how "full up" were we before this (latest) event hit. For example, how tired was I, how stressed was I about unrelated situations, or was there more to this latest situation than initially meets the eye?

Metaphorically, if you pour *half* a glass of water into a glass that is *one-fourth full*, the glass just becomes more full. If you pour that same *half* glass of water into a glass *three-fourths full*, water goes everywhere: it depends on how full the glass was before anything else was added. The same is true for each of us regarding our emotional capacity. If we are mostly "full" of stress, tension, or worry before more is added, any new stress or strong feeling might put us over the top. And yet, we are often surprised when we lose control.

HAVING FEELINGS IS ALWAYS OK, BUT HOW WE EXPRESS THEM MAY NOT BE
Like a quote by Lawrence Kincade

Once we decide feelings are not good or bad – they are simply feelings – we can consider all feelings are normal or human. Certainly, we may not appreciate all our feelings at any given moment, but we can clearly cope better when we honor our feelings - pleasant or not. There is a secondary concern about feelings which involves how we verbalize, act out, or express them. While we may try to justify *any* action resulting from a feeling, some of those actions are acceptable and some are not; in fact, some may be illegal. **My basic rule** is: any way of expressing feelings is ok as long as my behavior does not hurt anyone or anything (including me). For example, feeling angry about a situation is fine, ie, feelings are always ok. But, when someone decides to **express** anger by screaming at another person, or destroying something, or hitting his/her own head against a wall, these actions are not at all ok. They involve hurting someone – not ok.

Let's consider a classic emotional expression - "road rage." It is a feeling, right? Which makes it ok, right? No, I believe road rage is not a feeling, but rather a behavior resulting from intense, heavily fed anger. This anger is acted out in a clearly unacceptable way. Most likely, at some point, this driver had normal anger, which is ok. When the anger got fed and then expressed as yelling, cursing, threatening, and reckless driving, it is no longer ok. "Road rage" is very dangerous and can be life threatening.

85

ANGER FUNNEL

As a rule, men are taught not to show feelings in our society. For a man to feel afraid, surprised, embarrassed, sad, or hurt is taken as a sign of weakness. Anger has been "designated" as the one feeling that is ok for men. As a result of this, a curious thing happens in many situations: when other feelings occur to a man (such as fear, surprise, or embarrassment), he *changes those to anger* within seconds. It is as if the other feelings quickly went through a "magical anger funnel" that transformed them into anger ... the only acceptable feeling for a man. This funnel works so well, it only takes seconds and usually the man does not even realize what the original feeling(s) was.

As part of my approach to anger management, I have encouraged men to understand this anger funnel. Then, I urge them to recall a recent angry situation and go backward through *their* anger funnel for that situation. The idea is to help them find out what the feeling(s) was before it morphed into anger. At times, it may be necessary for me to offer suggestions or other help, by giving similar examples as illustrations. As they describe their situation and consider likely feelings (even "what other people might feel" in the situation), they can discover the feeling that was there at the beginning, before it became anger. Then, we can focus on dealing with that feeling(s), by first becoming comfortable with it (honoring it and owning it), and then deciding the best way to work through it, without resorting to the anger funnel.

BURIED FEELINGS NEVER DIE
Like a quote by Karol Kuhn Truman

In many ways, feelings are not valued in our intellectual society, as mentioned before. Because we have been told emotions make us weak and vulnerable, many people have learned to shove them down, STUFF them, or BURY them. If we can get rid of them in this way and keep a strong lid on them, we should be ok, right? And no one is the wiser.

However, when we stuff, shove, or bury feelings ... they just *stay* there. They never get resolved, and they never go away. Most likely, those feelings will surface again, probably at an inopportune time. For example, they might erupt when an event reminds us of the original cause for those feelings. Sometimes the feelings begin to leak out when we get filled up, and we can no longer keep the lid on. The feelings may leak slowly, as in a lower back ache, but they may erupt quickly as an unexpected, serious crying episode.. Rather than wait for a big, unpleasant surprise or a leak, we would do well to find out what we have buried and bring those feelings up. Then, we can work through them at a suitable time – for example, when we are *not* in a crisis or under lots of other stress!

EVERYBODY FEELS THINGS DIFFERENTLY

"I know just how you feel" is a common response people offer when someone talks about a difficult event. I think it is well-meant, but it cannot be true. Our feelings are personal, based on our complicated past, our family history of emotion, our years of "training" on the topic of emotions, and other similar experiences. No one can "know," and it can be insulting for them to think they can feel what *we* are at that time. I believe it is best to say to someone who is struggling, "I cannot know how you feel; I can only offer to support you as you work through it."

MANY "FEELING" WORDS ARE NOT FEELINGS AT ALL

Throughout our lives, we have been given mixed messages about the whole idea of feelings. While we are told *not* to feel, we are also criticized for not knowing exactly *what* we are feeling. We may have been encouraged to study lists of feeling words, to have a broad vocabulary about "feelings," which in turn will help us better express them. Unfortunately, many of the so-called "feelings" we were taught – even those found on *feeling lists* – are not feelings at all. Instead, many are **beliefs or thoughts about what we think has happened to us**, not how we feel about it. I will address this more in the next section (feeling and thoughts), but I want to clarify my point first. Words like "anger," "sadness," "loneliness," and "fear" are clearly describing true feelings. But, words like "slighted," "betrayed," "ignored," "dumb," and "worthless" are not feelings. Interestingly, I have often seen the second group of words in the blank: "I feel _____ ." Still, this wording does not make them feeling words. If you are describing a feeling, be sure to use a feeling word. (Check the next section for more about feeling words.)

MANY PEOPLE GET DEPRESSED, IN PART, BECAUSE THEY STOP DOING THE THINGS THEY ALWAYS ENJOYED
Like a quote by MacPhillamy and Lewinsohn

The **theory of pleasant events** asserts when people stop doing "pleasant events," ie, those things what they always enjoyed doing, they become depressed. And conversely, when people who are depressed start doing more "pleasant events," their depression lifts. Certainly, there are other causes of depression, and this idea is not meant to ignore that. Still, this can be a simple and powerful tool to help clients reduce and overcome depression. On line, there is a lengthy list, called **the pleasant events schedule,** which works well to suggest new activities or to jog people's memories about activities they used to enjoy. With over 300 specific events, the list includes small (gardening) and medium activities (getting a pet) all the way up to big events such as a Hawaiian vacation. Try it, you'll like it!

FEELINGS ARE CENTRAL TO GRIEVING

I have already mentioned my concern about our society's neglect of grieving. Here, I want to emphasize the central feature of grief: feelings. Rarely are grieving people given adequate support for grieving in our society, and if they are, the presumed time frame is too short, often just a few months. It should be closer to two years. For the record, the feelings associated with grief include . . . *everything*. Sadness is most common, but guilt, regret, fear, worry, and doubt are all present within grief. What's more, anger and relief can be part of grieving, too, and often these are harder to admit to or work through. I know even hallucinations can be present with some grief (hearing a deceased spouse cough or shuffle down the hall).

Grief can develop when someone loses *anything*. Unfortunately, much of this anguish is overlooked or dismissed as unimportant, because "that loss" somehow does not count. We tend to recognize grief only with death of a family member or close friend, but it is certainly broader than that. The loss of a job, starting retirement, losing a leg or a breast, the loss of a pet, or loss of independence - all can cause grief. The process of recovery is the same as if we lost a *person*.

From my therapy with many people, I have a standing concern about grieving people often not being given **permission to grieve**. Since their sorrow makes others uncomfortable, anyone grieving may be instructed to "Get over it," when they cannot. Sometimes, the grieving person is told to "keep it simple." Furthermore, this *permission* is greatly needed when a **past loss** piggybacks on a current one, making for a more extensive and confusing recovery. Finally, *permission* is essential when previously **stuffed** emotions become part of a new grief. Since *the right to feel* was not given originally, it is much more important this time around.

MAYBE YOU'RE HAVING ANTICIPATORY GRIEF

At times, I have had clients who were surprised to find themselves having very strong feelings even before a close relative or friend dies. In many cases, the person was disturbed by the feelings, thinking they were starting the grieving too early. While this may seem odd to many and may generate some guilt, such feelings are normal and are called anticipatory grief. These occur especially when someone is clearly in the final months or weeks of life, due to a known disease. Death is imminent and grieving begins when friends and relatives know the end is near. There can be another aspect to this, too: as the person declines, he/she may be unable to participate in the marriage relationship like before. The person may have stopped being supportive, stopped telling jokes, stopped planning events, etc. In a sense, the *relationship* that may already be gone. That's grief, too.

REGRET AND WORRY ARE LIKE PUTTING ONE FOOT IN THE PAST AND ONE FOOT IN THE FUTURE, THEN URINATING ON THE PRESENT

This graphic saying from AA reminds us we spend too much time thinking about the past and the future, which robs us of enjoying the present. One of the newer theories in psychology is called **mindfulness**, and it refers to staying in the present moment, acknowledging "now" feelings, and making the most of what this current time has to offer. After all, now is the only time I can clap, jump, hug, decide, learn, or . . . do anything.

Unfortunately, most of us have been well indoctrinated to **dwell** extensively on the past or the future, particularly with regret and worry. We have all been admonished to "hope for the best, but prepare for the worst," ie, worry. Some of us were punished with specific instructions: "I hope you will give a lot of thought to what you did and who you hurt, young man;" more focus on the past. We have been encouraged to analyze mistakes we have made (and the decisions we face because of them). The reality is, we cannot change the past and we cannot fix the future today. Why try? Besides, it seriously interferes with enjoying the present.

GUILT VS SHAME

When I was asked to give a workshop on this topic years ago to a group of teens, I started off thinking these two words were essentially the same. By the time I finished my homework, I saw them as different, especially considering the effect they have on self-esteem. "Guilt" is used to describe the temporary feeling when one has done something wrong, while "shame" applies to a strong and permanent black mark which makes the person wrong for what they have done. Guilt can be overcome and does not last forever, but, shame cannot be undone easily and often seems to stick, becoming a lasting characteristic or stigma for that person. "Shame on you" is a phrase used flippantly and often in our society, but unfortunately this saying can have a deep and lasting negative effect.

Without wanting to get into religion, I want to suggest a way to work through both guilt and shame, a method which results eventually in forgiving ourselves. If we do not work through the feelings, they can stick with us (maybe become "stuffed") and effect our self-esteem for years. To achieve our highest level of self-confidence, forgiveness is necessary. For this, we need to acknowledge the feeling, challenge any "beliefs" (thoughts) supporting it, unload any related feelings (for example, anger at the source of our shame), and find new perspectives to encourage positive feelings and self-love.

THE OPPOSITE OF LOVE IS NOT HATE, BUT APATHY
Elie Wiesel

"It is clear you still love her." "No, not at all, I hate her." This kind of statement implies love is over, the relationship is over, and the only feeling left is the opposite of love, ie, hate. But, hate is *not* the opposite of love, because hate involves a strong connection to the other person that still continues. This means love and hate

90

are similar, and both are based on staying "in" the relationship. **Apathy** is different, because it implies a clear **lack of relationship** - it is over. Oddly, many people who say they are "done" seem to enjoy the fight of staying in a negative relationship. Are you done? Or do you love to hate the other person – and stay connected?

This applies to more than romantic relationships. Sometimes, parents have relationships with grown children which can take this form, especially when control issues are at stake. In this situation, the parent is in a close relationship with their child, even though hate is the most prominent glue. Another example might be the children of a divorce: children are sometimes forced to choose which parent to agree with or support. As a result, love-one-parent/hate-the-other-parent may develop, and the parents are not willing to let this negative relationship go. This can be especially confusing for young children. A negative relationship can happen in other situations, too, such as when co-workers may slip into this awkward kind of holding on: no longer loving, but unable to let go, so they are miserably angry. I have also seen this when two people have hopes to rekindle a past "love." They prefer to hold on to a "challenging" relationship, rather than let go of hate and develop a **healthy apathy**.

This one-liner about feelings does not require an explanation:

THE ONE FEELING THE PAIN GETS TO DECIDE HOW MUCH IT HURTS.

Chapter 7

THOUGHTS AND FEELINGS

MEN ARE UPSET NOT BY SITUATIONS, BUT BY THE VIEWS THEY TAKE OF THEM.
Epictetus, First Century AD

THE SOURCE OF NEARLY ALL FEELINGS IS A THOUGHT
Like a quote by Aaron Beck

This is a **basic principle** of the many cognitive therapies. Feelings develop from our *view, perspective, interpretation, meaning, or thought* about a particular situation. This is why two people can look at the same painting or sunset and have almost opposite feelings. This is why we can have different reactions to the same situation on two different days. This is why some feelings can change so quickly – we only had to change our thought. The complexities of this idea are the substance of the different theories of cognitive therapy.

For clarification, I will repeat an important exception to this principle. Some feelings are on a more impulsive or instinctual basis, so they are triggered instantly by certain surprising, unexpected, or dangerous situations. This is part of our protective and valuable fight-flight response to perceived dangers. These feelings are an exception to this model, since the feelings are instantly protective.

THOUGHTS CAUSE EMOTIONAL PROBLEMS BY BEING:

UNFOUNDED AND IRRESPONSIBLE: Example: the thought "I never do anything right" is unfounded. For irresponsible: "Bad things always happen to me, so there is no use even trying." Both thoughts can lead to depression.

IRRATIONAL AND UNREALISTIC: An example of irrational thinking is "This rain is totally ruining my day." An unrealistic thought is "I am going to literally explode, if one more person looks at me negatively." These thoughts could easily produce anger or rage.

IMPOSSIBLE AND SELF-DEFEATING: An impossible thought might be "If I do not win the lottery today, I will just demand a rightful share of this week's winnings." A self-defeating thought could be "My mother - God rest her soul - was the only person who was ever honest with me. I can never trust anyone else."

STRONG FEELING HAVE TWO COMPONENTS
PHYSICAL AROUSAL AND A POWERFUL MENTAL LABEL
Schachter and Singer

This is an interesting theory of how emotions work, and I find it helps in understanding feelings and coping with them. According to this viewpoint, both components - physical arousal and a mental label - are necessary to have a strong feeling. If either the physical or the mental is missing, no significant feeling occurs. One "strong feeling" example: fear is the strong feeling, and it has a mental label (*thought*) that something dangerous is nearby; the physical arousal likely consists of an increase in blood pressure, pulse rate, or breathing. Depression can result from thoughts of being hopeless and helpless, which combines with loss of appetite, being tired, and changes in blood chemistry.

The value of knowing this view is the **information it gives to dismantle** any strong emotion. When we want to let go of a feeling or even moderate it, we can relax the physical side and/or change the thoughts attached to it. More specifically, to relax any high energy or use it up, we can take a walk, listen to quiet music, sit in a hot tub, try some light exercise, or even vacuum the floor. As for changing the thoughts, we can challenge the truth of what we were saying to ourselves or switch to another way of looking at the situation. Remember, changing either or both components results in a change in our feeling or emotion.

AWFULIZING AND CATASTROPHIZING CAUSE SUFFERING
Like a quote by Albert Ellis

One powerful way to understand how thoughts cause feelings is to notice how exaggeration magnifies any thought, making it stronger and more powerful. When the thought is magnified, it automatically magnifies the feeling, too. "Awfulizing" and "catastrophizing" involve just what the words suggest, *extreme exaggeration* in our thinking, which directly affects the resulting feelings. Then, our real suffering begins.

You may wonder exactly what awfulizing is? Here is an example: I received criticism from my boss about my last project (which is likely a *fact*) → I know he never liked my work (*a thought*) → I'm sure he is collecting evidence so he can fire me (a bigger, *exaggerated thought*) → he always has been a power monger (*a loaded belief*) → he's going to fire me to get in good with his boss (quite *exaggerated guess/ belief*) → then, I won't be able to find another job (*very exaggerated thought*) → I'll lose my apartment (*even bigger exaggeration*) → I'll end up on the street → and the rest of my life will be miserable...." As you may have guessed already, catastrophizing is quite similar to a train of thoughts.) This chain of thinking may seem to be an unlikely scenario, but many of us – yes, me too – struggle with this kind of thinking at times. What is most helpful to realize is when we can notice what we are doing quickly and begin to challenge our exaggerations, we can re-set our thinking to a more workable level, and a more reasonable feeling.

EXPECTATIONS CAN BE DANGEROUS

This idea was mentioned in Chapter 1, and now we explore it deeper. When we have expectations which do not fit with reality, we unwittingly set ourselves up for hurt feelings. Since our expectations cannot be met, we experience failure, and the result typically is negative feelings (hurt, disappointment, anger, and resentment). In each case, the feeling is not the *cause* of the suffering, but the expectation that came before it. In looking at our process this way, the feeling is 100% accurate for the thought or expectation we held to so tightly. As soon as we adjust our expectations, getting them more in line with what is likely to occur (ie, reality), any negative feelings are replaced by new, positive ones.

I have heard myself saying to clients all expectations were problematic. But, this is not true: **realistic expectations help us plan our lives, while respecting ordinary happenings, patterns, and events**. For example, expecting the sun to come up tomorrow, even if it is behind some clouds, is reasonable. Figuring, in Florida (my home state), it will rain on most days in the summertime is realistic. Guessing traffic will be heavier between 7 am and 9 am, and between 5 pm and 6 pm (Monday-Friday) is equally realistic (and beneficial to our planning).

The **trouble starts when our expectations become unrealistic**. Some examples might be: "My children must listen and do everything I say immediately," or "There absolutely cannot be rain on my wedding day," or "I must never make a mistake," or "my computer always saves all my work automatically." I hope the set up for failure and frustration is apparent with each of these expectations, because they are all glaringly **unrealistic.**

In all aspects of life, we benefit greatly by making our expectations realistic. This allows us to avoid setting ourselves up to try going against reality. One valuable way to do this is change any "should," "must," "have to," or "got to" - to a less demanding word. Try "wish," "want," or "hope." This lowers the demand level to be **lower and realistic**, which in turn allows success. An example: "I *should* get groceries first thing tomorrow" can be changed to "I *hope* to get groceries first thing tomorrow." The plan has not changed, only the pressure behind it. Another way to get realistic is to ask: am I being honest in our planning? An example of this might be starting an odd job at home on your day off. Am I being honest? Do I have the ability? Do I have enough time? *Planning realistically* helps avoid frustration – and other negative emotions. Being more realistic may involve challenging major, common beliefs about "perfectionism" and "people pleasing."

PROCRASTINATION AND DIFFICULTY DELEGATING ARE SIGNS OF PERFECTIONISM

Perfectionism is a way of life for many of us; we were taught this starting in our early years. "If you are going to do something, you might as well do it right." "I want you to give 100% out there today (or 110% or 150%)." "A's are nice, but don't they give A+'s in your school?" Unfortunately, those of us who have been exposed to and indoctrinated by the perfectionism bug often struggle with day-to-day tasks, both large and small, because we never seem to get them done well enough. Of course, the **unrealistic expectations or thoughts** associated with perfectionism clearly cause much failure, frustration, disappointment, and self-doubt.

In addition to these struggles, perfectionism gives us two surprising "corollaries." The first is **procrastination**. When we are worried we cannot do our best, we may put off a task until a deadline is upon us. At that point, the threat of not doing it at all is great enough to overcome our fear of not doing it perfectly - at least for most things. The second corollary involves **reluctance to delegate**: Since I try hard to do everything perfectly, "no one can do as good a job as I can, so I cannot pass this off to anyone else." Some of my clients did not know they struggled in part due to perfectionism, until I introduced them to these two corollaries.

LABELS

This particular way of connecting thoughts and feelings was introduced in Chapter 1, but deserves expansion. Simply put, labels are a specific kind of thoughts which often cause feelings. For example, we easily create emotional reactions any time we say or think: "That comment was stupid," "This task is impossible," "Last night was horrendous," "My boss is the worst," "Everyone is so greedy," "My neighbor is crazy," "This job is for morons." These labels seem to be used quite frequently in our daily life; did you know the power they have to cause serious negative feeling? My least favorite labels are "terrible," "awful," and "catastrophic." Like the labels above, it can be surprising how often these appear in everyday conversations, if we pay close attention. We may spout them *casually* - as a passing thought - but, somewhere in our brains, these labels register and create problematic feelings. Often, the issue in front of us is not that big, but truth is lost and the new perception is already imbedded in our minds. Now, our reaction

97

is in accordance with the "hugeness" of the labels we spoke or thought.

A recent example involved a woman who came into my office feeling bad; she immediately said her week was "intolerable." I quickly disagreed, saying her week could not have been "intolerable." She was surprised and insisted she had not yet described her week, so how could I possibly know. I told her she was *here*, so she must have "tolerated" the week somehow. As you can see, it is easy to **label** and then react to the label. So, how do we change this emotion-generating thinking? One way to soften our feelings and responses is to **notice these labels and challenge them;** over time, we can commit to throwing them out of our vocabulary and avoiding that trap in the future.

YOU JUST "SHOULD" ON YOURSELF

According to the noted psychotherapist and theorist, Albert Ellis, "should" is a bad word because it demands something that is nearly impossible. Since I have described this already, I want to add how I use this short saying with clients. After I have made them aware of the demand and pressure from this word, I simply repeat this saying to them. Then, I encourage them to identify how they used "should" and how it started to affect them. I also utilized the saying in a group I led; members of the group seemed to like being a little naughty and giving helpful feedback to others at the same time.

"SHOULD" HAS SYNONYMS

This point has been addressed somewhat already, but I wanted to review it briefly and clearly. The unreasonable pressure we put on ourselves with the word "should" can be achieved with other words, just as easily. Any word/thought which demands something unreasonable can cause suffering. The most common synonyms are "must" and "have to," but "got to" is rather common, too. Also, phrases like "you'd better" and "there's no reason you can't" pack the same likelihood of starting some unwelcome, strong, negative feelings. As mentioned before, substituting "hope" or "wish" in the same statement can make a world of difference in how we soon feel.

AUTOMATIC THOUGHTS

Here is an **important twist**. When we talk abut how thoughts interpret situations and cause our feelings, there is an implication we are aware of this process of thinking. This particular twist recognizes some of our thoughts are **automatic**: we do not initiate them consciously, and we are not typically aware they have occurred. Not aware, that is, until the feelings show up. The idea that thoughts cause feelings still holds true, but the process has most likely occurred "under the radar" and seemingly with a mind of its own. Still, these automatic thoughts can cause us to struggle.

Please know these thoughts can be changed, so more positive feelings are still possible. An approach I prefer involves figuring them out by **making educated guesses** about what the automatic thoughts might be. Sometimes, asking how another person might think or what hints a friend may have given can get us started. Once we have identified the automatic thoughts, then we can start to challenge, dispute, and dismantle the beliefs which are causing our strong reactions. At first, it might seem there are *no* thoughts and this whole idea - thoughts cause feelings - is wrong. With some practice and hints from what others have learned, <u>even these automatic thoughts can be identified, disputed, and changed</u>.

Again, an example may help. My favorite, which seems to affect many of us, is getting stuck behind a driver who wanders, slows down, speeds up, and then does it all over. For me and for many others, we "automatically" get annoyed and upset. If we look at this situation more closely, we can begin to guess and then confirm thoughts such as: "You are messing up everyone's day." "This is terrible, because now I'm going to be late." "You have no right to hog the road." "This is awful, because things are not going my way." "My whole day is ruined because of this." From these perspectives (automatic thoughts), it is easy to see why we become upset. At the same time, our new awareness (of what we did not see before) helps us to realize how we *can change our feelings by changing our thoughts.*

EVEN SELF-DEFEATING THOUGHTS CAN HAVE A "GRAIN OF TRUTH"

When we are clear how our thoughts cause our feelings, changing those thoughts becomes a natural and powerful way to feel better. We can do this by challenging such thoughts with some key questions, like: "Is this thought true?" "Is it helpful?" "Is this accurate?" "Is this working to my benefit?" "Is this an exaggeration?" "Is it especially negative?" By using these questions and others, we can begin to dispute the thought and eventually let it go.

Unfortunately, there is a catch: while these thoughts are clearly not helpful, they may contain some truth. This makes challenging them more difficult, and not so clear to dispute. For example, "I need everyone to love and approve of me" is a trap - it is absolutely not possible. Still, when we are in a work or social situation, being "liked" by others may make a difference when it comes to a promotion or to just fitting in. (Be careful here, some people would jump all over the "fitting in" one as not at all necessary, just desirable.) Thus, some people would insist this thought is true, at least in part. At that point, our best solution is to **downgrade the demand** we attached to being liked, by changing "need" (or must or should) to "want;" this allows us to honor the grain of truth, let go of the unhelpful demand, and still eliminate any strong, negative feeling.

HOLDING ON TO A RESENTMENT IS LIKE TAKING POISON HOPING THE OTHER PERSON WILL DIE
Nelson Mandela

Any bad feeling or thought of resentment I hold onto affects only me - not the other person. In fact, the other person may have no idea that I continue to be upset or that I was upset at all; then, that person would have no concern or struggle about my feelings. One might say my resentment is like a poison I have chosen to keep inside me, affecting me daily, but having absolutely no effect on the other person. And yet, what we typically hope is the other person will suffer greatly - or die. Clearly, that probably will not happen due to my hopes or holding on to resentment. Realizing this perspective allows me to choose to stop feeling badly, by letting go of the resentment. Holding on only hurts *me*.

FORGIVENESS IS LETTING GO OF THE HOPE FOR A BETTER PAST
Lily Tomlin

Forgiveness is a difficult task. But, as with resentment, not forgiving only affects *me*. There are many views about what it means to forgive: how you do it, when you do it, why you do it, and where forgetting fits in. Basically, forgiveness involves letting go of an old hurt, *and* letting go of the idea we can **magically fix the event - in the past.** When we refuse to forgive, we are banking on, "If I wait long enough, it will magically fix itself." The usual hope attached to this is the other person gets some proper punishment. Our belief typically is once "the wrong" is fixed, I will automatically feel better and I won't have to forgive. Sounds highly unlikely, you say? I certainly agree; a better plan is to accept what happened in the past, forgive that other person (for my benefit), and let go of the past, so I can move on and feel better.

"SELF, STOP"

Negative thoughts can plague anyone. Such thoughts can be random, persistent, past, present, totally fiction, or eating away at our core. Thinking them through or finding a good argument to defeat them may do no good. And, when they do occur, they may seem to hang around getting bigger and bigger. Unfortunately, if we allow this to happen, any negative feeling associated with the thought hangs around and gets bigger, too. One method to remove such thoughts (and feelings) is to forcefully say – out loud, if necessary – "**Self, stop**." This allows us to break the thought chain and shift our thinking to another, more positive idea ("thought substitution"). This can be a healthy reminder that I am in charge of my own thinking, and I am ready to get away from thoughts that just cause pain or sadness. To make this easier, it is helpful to have a list of good memories or up-beat dreams, so you can switch easily to one of them. These two, simple (but not easy) techniques are called **thought stopping** and **thought substitution.**

Undoubtedly, some people will argue we cannot stop what we are thinking, but, this presumes we don't have control over what we think. Really? If we don't, who does? This idea is another powerful concept at the core of cognitive psychotherapy: I *am* in control of my thoughts. We may not be accustomed to exercising control in a conscious and deliberate way. Now seems like a great time to practice.

HARMFUL THOUGHTS CAN BE IDENTIFIED AND DISPUTED

If we go back to basics for a moment, our perspective is we are "not upset by situations," but by our "views." Then, finding our self-defeating thoughts and challenging them is the best way I know to feel better. This sounds simple, but of course, it is not; and it is not easy. Some people have trouble with the basic concept (do feelings really work this way?), as well as difficulty recognizing the thoughts supposedly causing the upset. The **first step** is to practice with some common situations: begin by noticing the feeling, then the situation that "seems" to cause that feeling. The **second step** is to identify the thoughts (our thoughts) that interpret the situation and lead to the feelings. It may be easier to consider what thoughts people typically have and how these might be self-defeating. The **third step** involves challenging the thoughts, by asking are they true, helpful, accurate? This is referred to as disputing the self-defeating thoughts, and when we are successful, we are on the way to new, more positive feelings (and thoughts).

I AM SURE I WILL BE HAPPY WHEN

Our society seems to encourage this myth - a change in the world, my job, relationships, finances, health, or my spouse will automatically make me happy. "I must be patient, and wait for the stars to line up perfectly for me. Then, it will fall into my lap, without any effort on my part." This wishful thinking is another example of thinking that causes feelings: at first, these thoughts cause us to feel hopeful, but later we feel let down and sad – all from the same thoughts. There is great wisdom in realizing and thinking *nothing outside of me can make me happy*. Only *I* can do that.

"I FEEL LIKE ___" REFERS TO A THOUGHT, NOT A FEELING.

Many of us use this expression: "I feel like ___," fully believing we are talking about an emotion or feeling. But, in truth, this statement nearly always expresses a thought or belief, not a feeling at all. The blank is typically filled with what I think happened to me, or a label I thought fit the situation, or some other descriptive thought. As an example, "I feel like a fool" is not expressing a feeling, but a self-judgment. Or, "I feel like my best friend betrayed me" is voicing what I think has happened. A simple key to better understanding these statements is to ask, "How do I feel about _____." For these examples, "How do I feel about being a fool?" might be embarrassment. Or, "How do I feel about being betrayed?" might be anger. I would offer these are the *real feelings*. On the other hand, "I feel like ... a dunce ... a fake ... a sucker ...." all cite labels or thoughts, not feelings. If the question "How do you feel about _____?" leads to the same word, then it probably is already a feeling. An example of this might be: "I feel like I'm very angry;" asking "How do you feel about being an angry person?" the reply just might be "angry!"

CHAPTER 8

SELF-ESTEEM

HOW IS MY RELATIONSHIP WITH ME?

We talk a great deal about how important relationships are, but we seldom think in terms of "me having a relationship with myself." If we did, we might be asking ourselves how we are doing with taking care of "me." Am I showing myself kindness? Am I positive with *me*? Am I encouraging, supporting, nurturing to me, as I might do for others I care about? Unfortunately, the answers are often not so great. We treat ourselves much as we treat our families - we take ourselves (and them) for granted, and we do not give enough time or attention to them or "me." This may sound odd, knowing we live in a "me" society in the middle of a "me" generation, but actually we do not take care of ourselves well. We may indulge ourselves in things we want, things we enjoy, but we are not so good at giving ourselves things we really need to be healthy and content. This involves regular, intentional, and thoughtful **self-care**. As you can see, if I put no time or effort into nurturing myself, I will not enjoy a good relationship with me, because I will fail to do self-care.

DO NEGATIVES STICK TO YOU

I once saw a group of children put on a short play. Five or six youngsters walked to the front of the room, and each had "Post-it®" notes stuck to their shirts with words printed on each sheet. They read each other's' notes aloud: "stupid," "lazy," "stubborn," "no good," and "immature." Just then, another girl walked up, but she had no sticky notes on her. At first, the other children pointed at the new girl and whispered to each other. Then one approached the new girl and said, "You're different." She responded, "What do you mean?" The first child remarked, "You have no sticky notes on you," to which she answered, "That's right, they do not stick to me." After some disbelieving looks, several children pealed notes off themselves and tried to put them on her, but each note fell on the floor (cute trick for the children). "As I told you, *they don't stick to me*." How wonderful life will be when we all have the power to make negative words fall off or never stick in the first place.

SO WHAT AM I COMMUNICATING TO ME?

Most of us are quick to emphasize the value of our communication with other people, because this greatly affects the quality and closeness of those relationships. In "my relationship with me," how do I do with communication? What do I tell myself? With others we care about, we typically work hard to avoid accusing, arguing, being negative, or justifying. But, I believe we are not as careful with ourselves. In reality, we focus on negatives, nit-pick, accuse, and make excuses. We do not **tell ourselves positives**, such as "You're beautiful," "You make a great friend," "You have a terrific sense of humor." Maybe we would do well if we **communicated more intentionally**, especially more **positively** with ourselves. (See next section for how.)

NIT-PICK POSITIVES

I bet this expression sounds odd to most people. Many of us are familiar with "nit-picking" as it pertains to negatives, and the phrase rolls right off our tongues. Negatives have been a central part of our upbringing for most of us. We can easily create a long, detailed list of flaws in our appearance, behavior, beliefs, and achievements. And, when we are asked to describe ourselves, we seem much more comfortable naming the negatives, than in naming positives.

106

For a moment, imagine an old-fashioned balance scale, where you put an item on one side and enough known weights on the other side to make it balance. Got it? Now imagine you put all of your "nit-picky negatives" on one side of that same scale, and then put the few "positives" you can think of (or allow) on the other - it would never balance. There seems to be something wrong with this image. For all of us, I wish a better balance which requires finding many positives.

The solution, as far as I am concerned, is to do a better job of **nit-picking positives**. Give yourself credit for good things you have done for others - and for yourself. In the process, be as detailed, specific, and complete as you do when you nit-pick negatives. **Tell yourself it is ok** to count and acknowledge compliments, holding a door for someone, smiling at the person across from you (or the person in the mirror), listening, supporting, hugging (with permission!), noticing the clouds or rainbow, appreciating the sunset, washing dishes, etc. Take time to notice and count all the positives.

TRY BRAGGING ABOUT YOURSELF

Now, let us carry this suggestion a bit further, by bragging. *Bragging*? Oh, yes! I know, your initial response may be to consider this a despicable thing? After all, we have been told our head will swell, we will get "full of our self" and be obnoxious, we won't think of others at all, and our life will be ruined. But, please consider that it may be good for us to brag about ourselves. It might help us to **see and celebrate the good in ourselves**, and **develop confidence and self-esteem**. I think so, which makes this one of my favorite one-liners.

I would like to propose that there are two sources of brags – the good things we do for others and the good things we do for ourselves. The first group is valued in our society, so these are much easier to identify and talk about; we may even be able to give ourselves some credit for these – notice I say *some* credit. The second type of brag is much less acceptable and so they are harder to pull off; but, these are **more valuable to us individually**. When we **compliment ourselves** for the good care we give ourselves, we can definitely feel better. These brags also remind us what we can do in the future to take care of ourselves and to feel better then, too

Now, back to basics: most of us were taught bragging is bad, and turning this around can be difficult. Still, I believe it is a powerful ingredient of self-esteem - for young and old. By the way, bragging seems easier for children, since they have not been coached (brainwashed), yet, on proper social behavior. For them, "Mom, look at my beautiful picture," is easy and genuine. Unfortunately, our society will soon teach them to be more critical and not as "cocky." Clearly, one way to help this idea of brags is to encourage expressions of pride in children and each other. Another way to increase brags is to decide this is a legitimate and valuable way to feel better and then decide to start.

So, what are brags? "Brags" can be **putting into words anything good we have done**. Finally purchasing the car we always wanted, hiring a cleaning person, getting a pedicure (yes, you too, guys), and standing in the shower an extra 30 seconds to feel the relaxing "fingers" of the water are all good brags. Try it. Do something nice for yourself and acknowledge it with a brag.

TRY MAKING A LIST OF POSITIVE SELF STATEMENTS

Here is another extension of this idea of being positive to ourselves. This idea involves making a written list of positives we have done, so we can remind ourselves at any time that we have done much that is good. So, here are the rules. A positive self-statement (PSS) is an "I-statement" that is **(1) active, (2) positive, (3) specific, and (4) always true**. For example, "I am a compassionate person" is not specific, so it may not be true all the time (rules 1 and 4) - therefore, this is not a good PSS. By changing it some, it can be: "Last Thursday, I showed good listening with my 16-year-old daughter about losing her boyfriend." This statement is active ("...I showed..."), positive ("...good listening..."), specific ("Thursday" and "boyfriend"), and this example of being compassionate will always be true.

As you can see, general statements do not work, because we could easily refute them during a down time. This is what we are trying to avoid, by making the statements always true. Statements focusing on "lack of a negative" - "I don't smoke as much as I used to" - are also not good, since the focus is still on a negative. In a similar way, passive statements like "I received a nice raise from my boss" are not good PSS statements, because they say more about someone *else* than about *me*.

What about that "list?" Imagine writing many PSS over several months and then having this lengthy, black-and -white record of PSS at your fingertips. Then, imagine pouring over this "list" at a time when you are feeling down or sad or upset with yourself. Remember each PSS is non-refutable by design, so even a bad mood cannot discount them. This list becomes a great way to **remind yourself:** "I have positive qualities," and "I can celebrate those," and by doing so, "I can feel better."

GIVING OURSELVES "CREDIT" ONLY WHEN WE SUCCEED CHEATS US

In the Olympics, only the first three competitors in each event receive medals, and many people seem to think anything but first is "losing." I think we are missing an important realization here - someone who is fourth best in the world, or for that matter, sixth or fourteenth best in the world is amazing, because they are a big winner, too. Consider the amount of time spent training, the strict regimen of eating, sleeping, and exercise, and the other sacrifices they had to make along the way. I believe each competitor deserves recognition for their accomplishment – their success - even when they did not get gold.

The same is true for the rest of us in our everyday life. There are times we expend considerable effort chasing a goal and do not achieve it. Our goal may have been a promotion which was given to a co-worker, a new job which had 100 other applicants, an improvement in my health but the labs are no better despite being cautious, or winning at Bingo or bridge (when others wanted to win, too). There are always **many factors determining who succeeds** or wins, including some factors over which we have no control. Still, any time we expend an honest, thoughtful, valiant effort, I believe we would do well to give ourselves lots of credit. After all, in our own way, we did succeed, didn't we?.

"IT" OR "THEY" SEEM TO GET ALL THE CREDIT WHEN "THINGS" GO WELL

We have some odd expressions in our society. For example, when asked how we are doing, often our response is, "It is going well" or "Things are fine" or "Life is treating me well." Don't we mean **we** are actively making our life good by the choices we make and the activities we participate in? Then, why do we give the credit to "it," "things," or "life?" This likely reflects our training not to brag or think too highly of ourselves. Unfortunately, the effect of this is a subtle belief that good is there by chance or luck, never by **my intentions or hard work**. Plus, I apparently have done nothing to create or choose a good day. "The day" seems to have happened all by itself.

Another example of how we may not get credit involves our own oversight. On several occasions, I have asked my clients about positive events during the last week. I often received a response like this: "I got an unexpected call from an old friend." When I ask how this happened, the answer was usually "the friend called out of the blue." But, with further questioning, the client slowly discovered the truth - they called the friend twice in the past month and, when they got no answer, left a message each time. I believe the person in my office deserves the credit for this enjoyable experience - not their friend or luck – because it was not an "accidental" occurrence. When we can give ourselves credit for all kinds of daily efforts, we give our self-esteem a serious boost each time.

BOUNDARIES ARE ESSENTIAL TO GOOD SELF-ESTEEM
Like a quote by Rokelle Lerner

I have mentioned already the value of boundaries for several aspects of good mental health, particularly in relationships *and* with self-care. Well, since boundaries are often about self-protection, the value to self-esteem may be obvious. When we are able to take care of ourselves in a variety of situations, this provides a great deal of confidence. And when we can choose whether we will participate, share, say "no," or leave, this affords us much control, which is a part of having boundaries. On the other hand, if these rights and protections are missing, we cannot feel good about who we are or how we interact with the world. Some have used another word to describe this: empowered. I believe this is very close to self-esteem.

PREDICTABILITY AFFECTS SELF-CONFIDENCE

If we lived in a world that was essentially *unpredictable*, all our skills of observing, understanding, planning, and coping would be worthless. This kind of world would not respond as we expect; it would send us difficult "curve balls" with most or all activities. Fortunately, most of us do not face such a world. So, we are able to

110

develop skills that allow us to manage most situations, and in turn, we can develop a sense of confidence in those skills and ourselves. In this way, self-esteem depends partly on being able to predict our world.

It can be helpful to remember some people grow up – and even live today – in the kind of environment which is very unpredictable. It might be a world where parents are angry or abusive for no apparent reason, or they are generous without a reason, or parents switch back and forth with not reason or warning. In some countries, unpredictability may be the norm, where many people are totally clueless about physical or social safety. This kind of world can make anyone unsure of their ability to cope, resulting in low self-confidence.

HAVING "OPTIONS" IMPROVES MY SELF-CONFIDENCE

Any time I am faced with a problem, I look for options to help me solve it. In a situation where I see only one – or no – options, I often feel frustrated and defeated. But, as soon as I can **find or create or borrow more options**, I automatically feel better. Right away, I feel more in control, and, of course, I am able to solve the problem far easier. Surprisingly, this seems true even if I eventually pick the first/only option I had, from the beginning.

The significance of this idea is appreciating how options not only help me solve issues, they help me feel better in the process. Trusting there are **always options**, even when none appear at first, is definitely another key to self-confidence. Knowing we can brainstorm, consult a friend, ask an authority, or do some research reminds us options exist. Somehow, believing there are always options - or that new options can usually be created - can make a huge difference in how each of us feels about ourselves, our abilities, and the problems we face.

NEVER FAILING ONLY MEANS YOU NEVER TRIED
Albert Einstein

Failure is how we learn. It is totally natural for humans to experience failure as they try new things - there is no way to be good or perfect at something we have never tried before. But, if we do everything possible to avoid failing, like never trying anything new, then we deprive ourselves of new experiences, opportunities, and growth. Why are we so averse to failure?

Well, there is a major belief entrenched in our society which addresses failure: "You must be thoroughly competent, adequate, and achieving in all possible respects if you are to consider yourself worthwhile." Wow. Stated differently, it says you **must be perfect** to have any self-worth. While this sounds ridiculous, it still occurs everywhere in our society. When we realize this idea is **irrational and impossible**, we are better able to accept mistakes as part of being human. At that point, there is *no more self-criticism* for not "doing our best," not "being a little more careful," or "thinking it through fully first." It will be ok to make mistakes or to fail, because it is part of being human.

"AS LONG AS YOU DID YOUR BEST" -- IS AN IMPOSSIBLE GOAL

I have often heard this said to someone who was struggling or who could not achieve what they wanted. "Maybe you did not save your marriage, but it is great you did your best to try." "Don't get down on yourself for not getting that job, as long as you did your best." To put these comments into a new perspective, consider this: what percentage of my day do I really "do my best?" All things considered, I surely do "my worst" for some part of the day and" my average" for much of that same day. How much of the day did I actually do my best?

Let's look at this scientifically. If I were to make an old-fashioned graph of my "effort" over a period of several days, I would get what is called **a normal curve** (also known as a bell-shaped curve). That means my average effort would clearly show on the graph as occurring the most often, with my lowest level (my worst) and my "best" effort showing up much less often. According to this realistic view of daily effort expended, *no one can exhibit their "best effort" all the time*. Most of the time, we give a decidedly average effort. Insinuating someone should give their "best" all the time is an unreasonable goal and an unfair load to carry. Such *expectations* cause us unnecessary emotional pain, and I believe this is one expectation we all would do well to release.

STOP JUDGING YOURSELF BY IMPOSSIBLE STANDARDS

Expectations and impossible standards can be dangerous, as already mentioned. This occurs when either becomes unreasonable or impossible. Any time we evaluate our own behavior or performance using such unattainable goals, we are set up to fail. In turn, this failure reduces our self-esteem, especially if the failure occurs over and over.

An example could be meeting an important person unexpectedly, then getting tongue-tied. So far, no harm has been done: but, if we decide this reaction is "stupid and immature," we are in trouble. Our anxiety goes up and our confidence goes down. If we could only back away from this situation for a few minutes, we could probably remind ourselves such a reaction is quite normal. Unfortunately, we may start berating ourselves right away, losing self-esteem. A different example might be insisting to myself never to cry in public, because it is a sign of weakness. Well, there are numerous events that could occur in our life when tears would be considered **normal by most** people – seeing another person get injured, being injured myself, observing a lost parent (whose child is missing), attending a funeral, etc. Never crying at any of these events is clearly setting an impossible standard.

There are two familiar, **common standards** our society promotes for everyone, but both are definitely impossible. One is **perfectionism**, meaning we are never allowed to make a mistake. The other is **people pleasing,** meaning we are never to have anyone upset or disappointed with us. *Common?* Certainly. *Familiar?* Definitely. *Widely taught and demanded?* Absolutely. *Possible?* **Never**.

Another special area where I believe we judge ourselves and others by inappropriate standards is with *grieving*. (I alluded to this before.) Based on what I believe are *crazy ideas*, we are told to "get over it," quickly. *Forget about it, get back to normal, "buck up," move on.* Unfortunately, any idea grief is fleeting or easy to get past is definitely wrong. Judging ourselves by these **inappropriate standards** can only result - once again - in undue stress, unhappiness, and emotional pain.

BE CAREFUL HOW YOU FILL THE PROVERBIAL "HOLE" INSIDE

This is another example of the old idea of "not putting all your eggs in one basket." Emotionally speaking, many people experience a "hole" or aching inside themselves that needs soothing – an *emptiness that is self-esteem.* When we experience this, we are tempted to accept whatever comes along to fill the hole and remove the ache. A familiar solution is *a person,* and this seems wonderful at first, but later may cause more pain. Similarly, a job, a friend, a baby, "someone who needs me" may all seem to fill the hole. While all these ideas are tempting, *as the one wonderful, perfect way to fill the hole inside,* in the long run none will work. Relying on one special person or perfect job to feel good about ourselves can fall flat in an instant, if that **one item** filling our basket is lost; then, the hole inside is completely empty again. On the other hand, when we are able to **fill our self-esteem space inside** with a **variety** of supportive, nurturing people or a variety of positive activities, losing one is no threat. We can continue feeling good and doing well, in spite of the loss.

SMILE -- IT WILL MAKE YOU FEEL BETTER, AND OTHERS WILL WONDER WHAT YOU ARE UP TO

Most of us know a smile can be infectious, causing other people to smile. What we may not consider is how our smile - even if we are not in the mood - can cause us to feel better, too. Our attitude begins to match our smile. Laughter is similar to a smile, since it can be contagious, too. There is an exercise popular with teens, in which everyone lays on the floor, forming a circle, and putting their head on the next person's stomach. Nearly always, someone starts to laugh quite soon, then someone else laughs, then soon everyone is laughing. This can happen standing up, too, maybe in an elevator or other small area. So, with this in mind, let the smiles and laughter begin. Enjoy the contagion. It is bound to help you feel better.

"I HAVE STOPPED HEALING. NOW I'M JUST GROWING"

A client once shared this with me after many months of therapy. She told me she had a new realization after all of her hard work, dealing with poor self-esteem, family conflicts, grief, impossible goals, and stress. She was done healing, and now just wanted to grow. I found myself agreeing easily with her and feeling happy to have share in her success. I believe this happens often in therapy, when someone has made many changes in relationships, thinking, and coping. There may be more they want to achieve, but now they are not so eager or impatient. Now, they're simply growing.

"THERE AIN'T NOTHING YOU NEED TO KNOW THAT YOU DON'T ALREADY KNOW"

This is old time country wisdom, which contains a great deal of value. This bit of information came to me from an old therapist, who was able to appreciate both the education of therapists and the innate wisdom which clients have about themselves and life. According to this, all of us, especially our clients, can *stop desperately looking to a smarter person* for the answer to important questions. The answers are inside each of us, though we may not realize it. As a therapist, I am glad if I can guide clients in difficult times like these – and help them to discover answers for themselves. This may involve putting pieces together we or our clients have never "assembled" before. Unfortunately, there is a myth which says most people are incapable of solving their own problems or finding new solutions. It can be a beautiful discovery when people challenge the myth and find the power in themselves to heal.

Chapter 9

COMMUNICATION

PUT YOUR BRAIN IN GEAR BEFORE PUTTING YOUR MOUTH IN MOTION

We heard it as children, and this advice is still valuable today: "Take backs" may work in golf or pool, but definitely not in communication. Even in a courtroom, we know "The jury will disregard that last statement" does not happen. The best strategy, by far, is to **think before we talk.**

GOOD COMMUNICATION CAN BE CRITICAL

A man answered an ad for a painting job. He found the address and knocked at the front door. The man who answered told him the paint was around back, go ahead and get started. When the man finished and was getting paid, he said, "By the way, you don't have a 'porch', you have an Audi."

CLEAR COMMUNICATION ALWAYS INVOLVES RISK

When I counsel couples about communication, I warn them accurate, clear, revealing statements carry much more risk than vague, wishy-washy ones. Consider the following: "Are you sure you want to go to the mall tonight?" is safer than "I don't want to go to the mall tonight." If challenged about the first statement (question), one can always reply, "I was just asking." Being vague is an easy way to reduce risk when communicating; unfortunately, accuracy goes away with lowered risk. In my work with couples, lowering risk happens in many ways, like: "Maybe, if everything works out right and the weather holds, and I'm not too tired, we could consider going to the movie tonight, if it is a movie I want to see." *To be clearer* with this particular communication, which means *taking a risk*, the statement might be re-worded as: "I know you want to go to that new movie, and I'd be willing to go with you tomorrow." Riskier, clearer, and much better.

REFLECTIVE LISTENING IS A GREAT TOOL
Carl Rogers

We have all been told how important good listening is, but many of us were never taught how to *do* it. Reflective listening is one good way, and involves starting our response to another person with: **"It sounds like..."** or **"You seem to be saying...,"** and then "reflects" back the **main idea** and the **feeling** given by them. This prevents the listener from making disruptive responses, which would likely interfere with the sender giving a complete message. Common "road blocks" which disrupt the sender include interpreting, criticizing, judging, guessing, lecturing, or rushing to fix an issue. Reflective listening also allows the speaker to "hear back" what they just said, so they can confirm their message or make corrections. The following demonstrates reflective listening (ie, person 2):

Person 1: "I don't like it that the news is so negative and gruesome."

Person 2: "You sound frustrated with TV news."

Person 1: "Yes, I am, especially that NYC station with nothing good to say."

Person 2: "You seem angry with that particular way the news is reported."

Person 1: "Well, I wouldn't say angry, more ... disappointed."

Person 2: "I hear you saying you are unhappy with their report.

Person 1: "I guess I am, or maybe I'm just disgusted with the state of our whole world."

Person 2: "I see."

I have taught reflective listening in groups on several occasions. Inevitably, there is one person who hears the explanation and complains the technique sound like what a parrot would do. I have intentionally used reflective listening with that person, saying: "You seem annoyed that this just seems like parroting." At this point, as he/she goes on with the complaint, others in the room are quietly laughing. From their point of view, my reflective listening worked beautifully.

ACKNOWLEDGE AND CELEBRATE AGREEMENT

When two people talk, especially old friends or a couple, they seem to have a pact to keep their verbal interactions brief. Because of this, it seems that many important messages never get communicated at all. In part, this occurs because each one is silently saying, "You should be able to read my mind, since we have been together so long." Another belief that limits words is "You should know what I meant, without having to ask." But, *the never-spoken messages* which hurt the relationship the most are the ones that **recognize, acknowledge, and appreciate support and agreement**. Most of us just take this for granted, like so many other things in the relationship. When two people are able to acknowledge the fact they see something the same way, or have the same plan to address an issue, or appreciate the same movie (or joke, newscaster, viewpoint) **can greatly affirm the relationship**. But, so often the agreement goes unmentioned, and the shared ideas are not recognized. An opportunity to appreciate each other is lost. For couples who often disagree, the chance to *acknowledge agreement is important*. They can even celebrate, making that moment – and the relationship - much better.

IT OFTEN HELPS TO STATE THE OBVIOUS

This one-liner is an extension of the one above. As part of taking too much for granted and thinking the other person "should know" what we are thinking, we can forget to state what may be obvious to someone standing nearby – but not to our partner. Instead, we would all do well to stop assuming and *state clearly what may seem obvious.* Small responses like "I heard you," "I agree," "I understand" can be very beneficial, ie, no more guessing. Another way to think of this is honoring the other person enough to complete the communication. Other **obvious** comments include: "Thank you" (for listening, telling me, supporting me, etc.), "I disagree," "I don't know what to say," "I wish I could help," "I'm sorry," "You seem upset," "Do you want to talk?" The fact that these seem obvious is basically why they need to be spoken out loud: to complete the communication and confirm the message was received.

MEN AND WOMEN ARE DIFFERENT

Speaking of obvious, it is true men and women are different. Several books on marriage recognize when men have a problem they go off alone, trying to find a way to solve it. They usually seek out another person only if they are unable to find a solution themselves. On the other hand, when women are faced with a problem, they often seek out someone they can *talk* to about it, but they are *not yet* looking for a solution. Do you see the problem? In marriage, when a wife approaches her husband with a problem, she is probably *only* looking for someone to talk to. However, *he* assumes (from his own perspective) she is seeking a solution, so he eagerly gives one. As you might guess – or maybe you have experienced this yourself – since a solution is not what she wanted, she is now annoyed. She may even blame him for not being a good listener. He is proud of doing such a good job of "solving" her problem, but quickly gets negative feedback, which leads to confusion and frustration. Obviously, men and women need to recognize and respect their differences, and communicate those differences clearly.

MEN AND WOMEN ARE DIFFERENT -- PART 2

Do you know why Moses wandered for 40 years in the wilderness? "Like a typical man," he refused to stop and ask directions! (I have been assured a woman would have stopped.)

REACT OR RESPOND?

These two words may seem nearly the same, until we look closely at them. **React** means to act with little or no thought, which is a good way to handle something hot. **Respond** means thinking before you act, determining the best solution first. In conversations with others, especially our partners, we often react when it would be more helpful if we could pause, think, and then respond. It is hard to take back angry, hurtful words or actions, but this is often what happens when we react. The old adage of **"counting to 10"** before we open our mouths or speak angrily is just the ticket for these situations: finding a way to respond, not react, is better for myself and my relationships.

ACCUSE AND DEFEND.

At times when two people are talking, seemingly out of the blue, one person reacts defensively. Often, the other person wonders innocently, "What just happened?" Well, if we look closely, we may find an accusing question or statement occurred right before the defensive response. To an untrained eye, this can easily be missed; then, it seems the one person got upset for no reason. To really make a difference in this situation, recognizing the "accusing comment" becomes quite important. This helps the two people understand clearly: **accuse ✳ defend**. So, how does this happen so innocently? There are two great communication **accusers**: "Why" and "You." Starting a sentence with either of these words almost guarantees a defensive response. Adding "always" or "never" increases the power of the accusation, even though the speaker may not realize what they did. Examples of these would be: "Why are you always late?" or "You never give me a straight answer when I ask you a question." Either of these communications could easily, almost automatically, generate defensiveness.

To confuse matters, we are told the best defense is a good offense (attack). But, a "defensive" come-back to an accusation continues or intensifies the ill-fated conversation, maybe over and over. Each person is free to believe the other started it ... and is the guilty party. As a result, neither person accepts responsibility or feels a need to apologize. Predictably, the argument worsens or the cold shoulder starts, often with both people completely unaware of what happened.

"THAT SOUNDS LIKE CRAZY-MAKING CRAP"

This is one of my favorites. Years ago, a client in Oklahoma wanted to move back to Denver where her children and grandchildren lived. But, her husband, who was comfortable on his small Oklahoma "ranch," always talked her out of it when she brought it up. Eventually, she had a revelation and realized he was "feeding me crazy-making crap." When she shared this with me in our next session, I confessed it was a new one for me. She offered this to clarify: the reasons he used to convince her were **crap**, because they were absolutely not true - she *did* want to pick up her grandchildren from school, *see all* their games and performances, and get "stuck" with them spending the night. Furthermore, she explained his arguments were **crazy-making,** because he was so convincing and emphatic, she doubted herself each time they talked about it. With her permission, I am pleased to present her one-liner here. By the way, she soon informed him she was moving back to Denver and he could go or stay; he decided to go, too. The big question is: "Who is feeding you crazy-making crap? What will *you do* about it?"

BLAMING THE OTHER PERSON DESTROYS GOOD COMMUNICATION

This is probably another fairly self-explanatory saying. Blaming, finding out who is at fault, noticing who "started it," or starting off angry all make a mess of communication. Ideally, when we communicate, we begin as two people "on the same team," with both desiring to find a satisfying answer, so a problem is solved. Much of the time, these basics get lost, and we become opponents desperately trying to insist on getting our own way. Blaming seems to be a powerful tool to achieve our own agenda, but, it works poorly when we hope for good communication.

"BUT" ERASES EVERYTHING COMING BEFORE IT

But is a word on my most-dangerous word list. Listen carefully to conversations, and you will see: each time it is used, the idea before the word "but" gets cancelled out. Still, we use it often, and seldom do we realize the effect it has. "That dress looks nice, but it doesn't fit you very well." Then how can it look nice, or are you saying it would look nice on someone thinner? "I agree with everything you said, but . . ." How can you agree, if you immediately begin your counterargument? "You look handsome, but your clothes look like they came from a second hand store." How can *handsome* be true?

I believe "but" is sometimes used when we have something negative to say. We try to soften the negative by putting a positive, first. Usually, the other person can see through this, knowing the important information comes after the "but." I strongly urge clients to avoid the word, since at the very least it confuses the message. We can do this easily by making two separate, independent statements. Leave out the but entirely. Or, we can insert an "and" between the two statements: in this way, we are honoring both statements and exercising a little tact. Hopefully, this gets us a better response from the other person. A simple example would be "I really think that outfit looks great on you, but there is a stain on the waist in the back." This could be replaced by "I really think you look great in that outfit. I am not sure you know there is a small stain in the back today."

"JUST" IS A FOUR-LETTER WORD

This is yet another word on my most-dangerous-words list.

- "Just do it." (from Nike)

- "I don't see why you don't just..."

- "It's not that complicated, just . . ."

- "I know you are afraid, but you just have to . . ."

These statements minimize the difficulty of the task, implying there is no problem. These statements ignore our reservations and disregard our intuition. There can even be a strong hint to "Just do it because I say so."

The truth is, many tasks we face are not easy, even if we (or someone else) wants them to be. Making it *sound* easy does not change the fact the task may be difficult, often for a variety of reasons. Any time we retract the word "just" in our communication, we demonstrate more acceptance of the task and the other person. Honoring the other person's reasons allows us to *listen better*, as well as offer to help them work through reservations or fears they have. Otherwise, we are likely to slip into a position of an opponent or dictator in our communication and problem solving with others.

MIND READING -- RIGHT OR WRONG, I DON'T LIKE IT

"Mind reading" - and telling the other person what you have "read" - is a no-no. This often happens when someone does not respond quickly enough or fully enough: the listener jumps in with their best guess. Mind reading may also occur when the other person does not give the answer we were expecting. In each situation, if we begin to guess what the other person is "really thinking," we really are intruding on their thoughts. When we do, they are likely to become defensive, and the communication goes downhill: "If I wanted you to know, I would have told you."

A few years ago, I was wrestling with this myself. I realized when someone read my mind and they were wrong, I did not like it at all. But, I also realized if they read my mind and were *right*, I still did not like it. At first, I was surprised; then I accepted for myself, whether right or wrong, mind reading is definitely offensive to me. I am fine if the person *asks* what I am thinking, because this lets me decide if I am ready to tell, how much I may want to reveal, and whether I am willing to take the risk.

"I'M FEELING DEFENSIVE, AND I DON'T KNOW WHAT TO SAY"

When a discussion turns negative, I believe stopping the ongoing negative interaction is crucial for the best health of the relationship. This can be quite difficult if each person has more to say on the topic, or feels a need to put in one more jab, or "just" needs to explain that last comment. When either person decides to stop the negatives, one gentle, powerful way to do this is to **take the heat personally and admit his/her own defensiveness.** The one-liner above is one way to help break the cycle of accusation and hurt. In actuality, the full statement probably goes more like this: *"I'm feeling defensive and ...* **I can think of lots of yukky things to say, none of which would be helpful right now, so** ... *I don't know what to say."* As you can see, the condensed version is honest, it is an "I" statement, and it does not put more fuel on the fire. This is exactly what I believe the relationships needs to end negativity and to make the communication more constructive; this response helps us stay away from the common responses which so often escalate situations. Remember, nasty words cannot be taken back, and some people have very good memories.

TAKING A "TIME OUT" CAN HELP DIFFUSE TENSE COMMUNICATIONS

Another way to avoid harm in negative conversations is to call a **time out** (TO). The idea is similar to sports, where a time out is a way to stop the game, re-group, strategize, cool off, or slow things down. In communication, a time out can help greatly to avoid hurtful statements. The official process is: (1) either person can call TO, (2) both people stop immediately, with no parting shots, (3) they separate, out of sight and hearing (*not* in the same room or nearby), (4) each person **takes responsibility to cool himself/herself off**, and (5) they come back together – when both are ready - to finish the conversation calmly. It may happen that one person could be ready to continue the discussion before the other. Wait until both are ready. There is **no time limit** on TO, since every person is different in how quickly they can cool off, re-group, and approach the topic calmly.

Next to stopping any hurtful statements or accusations, the most important part of TO is **cooling off**. This is each person's **own** responsibility, and it means finding ways to let go of hurt, anger, blame, retaliation, stubbornness, and tunnel vision. TO also means beginning to refocus - on resolving the problem with this person you *usually* appreciate. Cooing off allows us to let go of the need to express our feelings and solutions loudly or emphatically. This lets communication work for both people.

TRY WRITING A NOTE

There are times when attempts to communicate difficult issues *verbally* do not work. If we try, we may get interrupted, we may lose track of our key points and not finish, we may get defensive, or we may word something in a hurtful way. At those times, a helpful option may be to express our opinion and our relevant reasons on paper. This way, we can write it several times until we get the wording just right, we can show the other person at the beginning how much we have to say, and we can be sure not to forget any important points. In addition, the other person is not required to respond immediately, so they may be less likely to reply impulsively or defensively. Once the note is done, we have options to hand it to the other person and wait, or read it to them, or send it to them as an email, or leave it for them to read later (see hit and run, below).

TRY "HIT AND RUN"

Sometimes face-to-face communication is too risky for a hot topic. Still, being able to address and resolve it may be a high priority. One idea (see above) is to write down what it is we want to say. Then there are several ways to present it to the other person. If we choose to lay it where the other person is likely to see it and then leave the premises, I refer to this as **hit and run**. When you return later (maybe 1 to 2 hours), the other person has had uninterrupted time to read and digest, maybe vent some feelings - all without your being there. The value of hit and run is the communication can be more successful afterward. Another way to do this is to make a brief, clear comment and then walk away, maybe staying nearby to be available to address the issue quickly. I do this with my daughter, because she often responds so quickly and so sharply, our communication is off to a bad start before we get to start.

PLEASE VENT TO ME, NOT AT ME.

This insight came from another friend. When her husband came home from work, she enjoyed hearing about his day. He often expressed frustration with fellow workers or rules, and she was happy to be a sounding board. However, there were times when his frustrations took a twist - and were **aimed at *her***. She knew she was not the cause of his frustration, but he sure made it seem like it. When she gently reminded him he was aiming at her, he readily backed off - and usually even apologized. I suspect our partners do not mind helping us blow off steam or frustration. But, as soon as our blast is directed at *them* (not the person who caused the feeling), we hurt the one who agreed to help us vent in the first place. So, remember with any partner you love and respect to vent *to* him/her, not *at* him/her.

TRY "BROKEN RECORD" TO HELP GET WHAT YOU WANT

One of the most well-known suggestions coming from assertiveness training is a technique called **broken record**. Much like vinyl records (from the old days) which got stuck and repeated the same stanza of music over and over, this technique consists of someone saying the same thing repeatedly. This avoids getting caught up in the other person's explanations, excuses, questions, and distractions, allowing us to stay on the point: "I still want what I want." The best kind of broken record is a fairly neutral, non-blaming, clarifying statement of what I want.

A classic example involves getting your car back from the mechanic, but it has the same problem as when you brought it in. If you give up and decide to forget about it, you are being "passive." When you are passive, you simply do not get what you want. On the other hand, if you yell and threaten, you are being what is referred to as "aggressive," and this is likely hurting the other person. (For people who use aggressive ways often, they often do not care if others do get hurt.) Instead of either of these ways of handling a problem situation, being **assertive** using the **broken record can be quite helpful.** This involves attempting to get what you want without hurting anyone else. In the example of your still-broken car, you might quickly take the car back to the mechanic and say, "I need my car fixed." (This is a calm, neutral, non-blaming comment.) If the mechanic says, "Sorry, the guy who worked on your car just left for lunch", your response is – predictably - "I need my car fixed." If the mechanic next says, "We are pretty busy and cannot get to it now," we could say again, "I need my car fixed." Another distraction by the mechanic might be, "It will probably cost more than you are ready to pay. "I need my car fixed." "Well, you really need a new car, anyway" meets again with "I need my car fixed." This technique keeps us from getting side tracked, becoming demanding, defending ourselves, getting angry, or walking away frustrated. If after several repetitions of this wonderful phrase there is no movement, it is ok to decide on another approach, like bring in a friend, consult a lawyer, just sit down and wait, or call the owner's wife and cry on the phone (just kidding). For many situations, using broken record can greatly help us get what we want. It is sure worth a try. By the way, practice helps: people who use broken record gradually get better and experience more success.

"YOU AND I HAVE A PROBLEM WE CAN'T RESOLVE; WHO IS YOUR BOSS?"

From yet another friend, I learned this specific example of using **broken record.** He was returning something to a department store, but the clerk insisted she could not give him his money back. After some discussion, his statement was: "You and I have a problem we can't seem to resolve. Who is your boss?" She pointed him to the department supervisor, and he explained his problem again. When she, too, insisted she could not return his money, he simply repeated, "You and I have a problem we cannot resolve. Who is your boss?" Eventually, his trek took him to the store manager, who had the same response and could not help, either. *His* boss turned out to be the regional manager. When my friend asked to get them on the phone, the store manager suddenly decided he could help after all - and returned my friend's money. That's a lot of **broken record**, but it worked.

Some people might call this "persistence" or "assertiveness," and some might say it is clever; but, others would say it was obnoxious. Whatever you call it, it got his money back - in true assertive fashion of **not hurting himself or anyone else**. The simple fact it worked - and hurt or insulted <u>no</u> one - is valuable to see. For use at home with a family member, it can still be wise saying this a few times; then, calling time out if there is no progress may be better than saying the broken record fifteen times!

"IT" -- YOU KNOW WHAT I MEAN.

No, I probably do not know what you mean. The word "it" seems to be used quite often and can refer to most anything, including people, thoughts, art or events, or even the last thing I was talking about. When we are trying to communicate accurately, this word can be quite confusing, while at other times may serve well. The problem is the speaker assumes the listener knows exactly what "it" means in the present conversation, so sees no need to clarify. But, this may not be true at all - especially if there are several different "its" that might be the "the right one."

Another interesting aspect about this word is how "it" allows us to avoid saying certain words we are actively trying to never say. This may be done to avoid feelings attached to a particular word, or even to avoid saying the feelings themselves. For example, some people talk about "it" meaning "sex:" but, using the word "it" helps us avoid embarrassment. "It" can also refer to our sexual organs, or a bowel movement, a pimple, a nasty rash, a bad hairdo, or a frustrating ex-relationship. More broadly, some concepts have been linked with uncomfortable feelings, and these can be avoided by using "it:" for example, death, cancer, euthanasia, severe world hunger, the holocaust, and modern day slavery might be **too uncomfortable** to say out loud. One final thought, "it" can be an intentional sort of **code**, used so only some people know what "it" stands for, and others are left out of the inner circle.

If grief is the "it," we may try to avoid the death or loss, as well as uncomfortable feelings that are a natural part of grief. It then becomes one more method we can use to avoid, stuff, minimize, joke about, or get some distance from our feelings - often because the feelings affect us so deeply. Unfortunately, not naming the current feeling only postpones the grief, and prolongs the grieving process. Other avoidance words often used with unwanted feelings – and grief, particularly – are "he," "she," and "they." This is to avoid saying the name of the person we lost or from naming the feelings; again, sidestepping grief.

YOUR "FACTS" FEEL LIKE ATTACKS

When others claim to know the truth about something, they may use their "facts" to <u>argue for</u> their idea and against my idea. It is quite possible their **facts** are *strongly stated opinions*, not facts at all. When such an opinion is presented as a "fact," **the intent** may be to "win at any cost," by incorporating power, framing the problem with blame, and then heaping on guilt. What seemed in the beginning to be a "factual" observation or concern about me, was probably an *attack in disguise*. When this happens in a conversation, my job is to recognize what is actually going on, so I can protect myself, now and later I would be wise to discern the other person is not a friend, and their words are not helpful to me.

APOLOGIZE VERY CAREFULLY

Good apologies can be powerful in relationships, and "worth their weight in gold." But, apologies can be difficult to accomplish successfully. First, if another person believes an apology is needed, whether I give it or not deserves serious consideration – do I agree? Do I believe it will help? What about saving face? Second, choosing the right words, the best time, and a genuine non-verbal expression have much to do with a successful apology. Third, if I choose to apologize, I need to focus on what the person is complaining about, whether it was intentional or not, addressing their complaint, *without* excuses or explanations. Fourth, talking *around* the hurt does not work, because it implies I am taking no responsibility for what happened. Instead, being specific about what I did works better.

The fifth idea about apologizing gets somewhat tricky: if I really *do not believe I did anything wrong*, it still seems wise to offer an apology *for accidentally hurting* the other person with what I did (which was ok in my mind). This means expressing genuine regret that the person was hurt by something I did – certainly, I did not intend to hurt them, so I can be truly sorry! Try this example: to say I am sorry

129

for voicing my opinion could be what the other person wants, but it would be insincere. Instead, I may apologize by being genuinely sorry for stepping on their toes (with my opinion) or refusing to hear their opinion (which hurt their feelings).

Consider this example: person #1 says, "You hurt my feelings when you criticized my outfit." Person #2 is sure he/she did not "criticize," but decides to offer this apology, "I am sorry I hurt your feelings with what I said about your outfit." Notice person #2 did *not* say, "I did not criticize your outfit," nor "I am sorry you took offense at what I said," nor "I am sorry I criticized your outfit." All of those responses would have hurt more and/or been a lie. The first response allows person #2 to give a genuine apology, without admitting to something the person *did not believe* he/she did.

Since this is difficult, let's try another example: Person A says, "I guess you were trying to make me sad, by reminding me this is the anniversary of my mother's death." According to the list above, <u>first</u> I believe it is to my advantage to respond to this in some way. <u>Second,</u> right now would be a good time, and not joking would be a good affect. <u>Third, fourth, and fifth,</u> if person B did not intend to sadden person A, maybe this would work: "I am so sorry that my reminder makes you feel sad."

THE BEST DEFENSE IS A GOOD OFFENSE ... ARE YOU SURE?

This interesting idea has been around a long time. In communicating with someone whom I consider special, I definitely do not agree about going on the offensive; I would never encourage it, because it sets up a fight. If I did attack another person (a good offense), then I believe our discussion will be negative and will not go well. Either my behavior will shut the other person down (no communication), or they will become defensive, and counter-attack. My offensive stance is <u>neither risk-taking nor honoring</u> of the other person. The best approach is to honestly state my own defensive feelings.

Is there ever a time to use this idea of a good offense? In a situation or relationship that means little or nothing to me, I might consider this a way to terminate a bad, unwanted conversation. Still, the other person may respond badly, causing more problems. Even in this situation, stating I do not want to talk or walking away may be better.

RESPECT PROVIDES THE FOUNDATION FOR COMPROMISE

We have discussed the importance of respect, even for compromise (Chapter 4). To review briefly: when two people are trying to make a decision together, they may easily disagree about details, as well as about the best overall solution. Working toward a compromise is the obvious answer, but this will never happen without **mutual respect**. This respect allows each person to state their view, listen to the other person's view and honor their perspective, and eventually find a solution - perhaps "between" their separate ideas. Without respect, neither person has a reason to listen to or honor the other's "ridiculous," "selfish," or "ignorant" opinion. This ensures <u>no</u> compromise.

LET'S AGREE TO DISAGREE

This one-liner is related to respect (above) and is another basic requirement for good communication and problem solving. Since people are different, their ideas and solutions are bound to be different, too. If they argue endlessly about which view is "most correct," or who is "right," no decisions will be made and no problems will be solved. A **change in perspective** may help: "you probably believe you are right in the same way I believe I am. So, neither of us is ready to give in to the other." When we can utilize this perspective and stop trying to sway the other person to our viewpoint, peace is possible: we can agree to disagree.

WHAT ARE YOU SAYING?

There are many ways to have **negative or unclear communication**, as the one-liners above attest. Another common way is to send a **mixed message**, in which two opposite messages are included in one communication. An example of this is to say with a loud, irritated voice: "I am not angry." Clearly, this sends two messages at once. Another method is to include an "if" in the middle of our sentence, which weakens our statement: "I could go with you to visit your mother, if we can be sure we do not stay too long." Confusing – are you willing or not?

Another frequently-used method which confuses communication is **hiding a statement in a question**. In this method, the sender can avoid stating what they want to say but hint at it with their carefully worded question. An example would be: "Are you sure you want to go to the mall tonight?" This way, if the sender is challenged about what he/she meant, the sender can say he/she meant nothing by it at all - it was just a question. While most of us might believe the sender is saying he/she does not want to go, the sender might side-step with: "Why, what did you think I meant?" (Cute, yet another hide-the-statement question.)

Once, while doing couples therapy, I was told by a young husband, that – as a salesman – he was taught to never answer a customer's question directly. Instead, he was to get more information first, by **asking more questions**. Unfortunately, the husband used this technique at home with his wife, and she did not like it at all. Instead, she wanted simple, clear, risk-taking answers to her questions. I certainly agreed this would facilitate good communication, but it was hard for him - and for her.

THAT'S CALLED KITCHEN-SINKING IT

In any problem-focused conversation, good communication suffers greatly if we bring up issues from the past (whether unrelated, similar, or unresolved). Bringing in other side/irrelevant issues can disrupt good communication, too. This poor style of communication is referred to as "kitchen sinking it," because we bring in everything but the kitchen sink. As you might guess, this confuses the discussion, making it impossible to address any one issue, especially the initial one. If this happens repeatedly, there is a strong likelihood many problems never get resolved and are "stashed away." Of course, these then exert an even greater negative effect on the relationship, and such hidden issues are ready to pop up during future communication.

EXPLANATIONS DO NOT CHANGE ANYTHING

This is another problem I have observed in everyday communication: the frequent use of explanation, justification, rationalization, and excuses. Each of these is meant to strengthen the speaker's own position or point of view, making them right or free of responsibility. Then, they can more easily insist the other person must see things their way. Unfortunately, this rarely works, and the communication stops and the relationship suffers. The other person may cave in or they may get stubborn, either of which is bad for the relationship, with the two people locked in a power struggle and neither person willing to budge. Correcting this involves stopping all explanations, rejecting any attempt to dominate decisions, being willing to take risks, and honoring the other person's ideas.

TO BE SAFE, SAY NOTHING AT ALL, RIGHT?

Sometimes, expressing our own ideas or opinions seems too risky, because it causes serious disturbance in a relationship. For anyone who tries hard to avoid upsets and risk, it is tempting to not answer questions, not volunteer one's view point, not disagree, and not make a request. If one is clever, a disguised way to do this is to **qualify** – talk without saying anything definite. This can be done easily by using "maybe," "if," "possibly," "depending," or "We'll have to see." One of my personal favorites is: "We could go to the movie tonight, if the parking lot is not too full and there will not be any rain, and depending on the times the movie is shown, and if the kids don't need a ride somewhere, and only if you are sure this is the movie you really, really want to see." Wishy-washy and saying nothing.

In using such words and expressions, the speaker is vague enough to avoid being held accountable for anything. They are safe. Unfortunately, their voice is lost, their point of view is never considered, they are overridden, and their communication is quite poor; but, of course, they are safe! For some people, this has become their way of life, because the relationship is not safe for them to say what they think. For these people, it may be time for a relationship overhaul, a new injection of self-esteem, or a new relationship.

ACTIONS SPEAK LOUDER THAN WORDS

We all know this saying, but what does it mean about communication? Research shows when there is a difference between actions and words, people believe any non-verbal communication before they believe the meaning of the words. "I'm fine," said when I am fidgeting or tearful, means the words are probably not believed. When we are trying to communicate clearly and accurately, our inflections, tone, volume, and body language all communicate, too. If there is a discrepancy, actions are trusted, first.

These one-liners about communication require no explanation:

SOME THINGS ARE BEST LEFT UNSAID

PICK YOUR BATTLES WISELY
C. JoyBell C.

IT IS BETTER THAT OTHERS THINK YOU ARE A FOOL, THAN TO OPEN YOUR MOUTH AND PROVE IT
Like a quote by Abe Lincoln

CHAPTER 10

GROWTH

NO REAL GROWTH COMES FROM SUCCESS; GROWTH COMES ONLY WITH MISTAKES
Like a quote by Linda Ronstadt

This is a tough idea to accept, because we all like success, and we strive for it daily. But, if we stop and think about it, success does not teach us anything. There can be times when we are "successful," but do not know why - what did we do to make that go well? What did we learn from it working well? When we pursue success, we try hard to avoid mistakes. Oddly, if we could accomplish this, we may never learn anything – there would be no mistakes to show us what to change. A story about Thomas Edison has a reporter noting he failed ninety-nine times when making the first light bulb; why did he keep trying? Edison responded he learned ninety-nine ways that did *not* work, and each put him closer to the idea that *would*. His failures led to success.

For most of us, this idea calls for a serious "paradigm shift." We need to find a new way to look at success and failure. We can start by putting less emphasis on doing everything right the first time, and more emphasis on what we can learn from each mistake we

135

make. We could all benefit from giving ourselves **permission** to experiment, so we can discover what does <u>not</u> work, as well as what does. Life surely would be different.

Years ago, I read about an experiment evaluating what people learned by watching someone model (demonstrate) an unusual task. The set-up utilized two models solving the same task: one did it easily and correctly on the first try, while the second struggled and made many mistakes, but finally solved the task. Separate groups of subjects observed the two models, and then each subject performed the task alone. The group members who saw the struggling model did better when it came to completing the task on their own. Clearly, they learned from the model's mistakes and successes, benefitting from both. Maybe it is time for all of us to embrace "failures" - or learning experiences - as a good thing.

CHANGE TAKES TIME AND INVOLVES TAKING RISKS

We probably all know this bit of wisdom: rarely does change happen quickly, and few things change without someone going into "unfamiliar territory" without a guide. We may *wish* change could be instantaneous and easy, but our experience tells us it will not be so. Even learning to ride a bicycle took all of us a while, and involved trial and error, as well as scratches and bruises. *Hoping we can grow without making mistakes or sticking our neck out is not likely to help.* "Edge walkers" are the people who often move forward the fastest, probably because of their awareness of the need to risk and their willingness to do just that.

TIME DOES NOT HEAL ALL WOUNDS

We know that, physically, wounds need time to heal. But, they also need to be kept clean and given good care. Emotionally, time alone does not heal, either. People who have been emotionally wounded, and want to heal, need time - and much more. They need protection from re-injury. They often need help or guidance from someone they trust to see the wound differently, so they can let it go, effectively and permanently. Getting this help may require giving themselves permission and freedom to heal, some understanding of the injury, and even specific tools to use to heal.

In many ways, **growth** is the same. We might *dream* of a machine "implanting" new skills, competencies, or even new experiences, but that only occurs in fiction. Making the changes necessary to allow us to grow, learn new skills, and hone that growth requires time, practice, correction, and confidence. Time alone does not provide enough for us to experience growth, or healing.

WHAT IS YOUR GROWTH ATTITUDE -- ARE YOU OPEN TO LEARN?

I believe most of us see ourselves as always being ready to learn. In many ways this attitude is what made America strong and what got most of us where we are today. But, when we look closely, the truth may different, and we might be closed or cautious about growth and learning:

- we may be afraid or short on confidence, knowing there is a risk.

- without realizing, we may have convinced ourselves we know all we need to know.

- we may find no use for some particular information at this time, and "pass."

- we may overlook an opportunity right in front of us to learn, by not paying attention.

We can often learn from children, because they have an unbiased, fresh, inquisitive approach to life; you know, "Out of the mouths of babes." But, *we* have to be open to *notice* what they say and do, and then pay attention to actually grasp it. Similarly, many people would insist there is much to learn from nature – just be quiet and observe. Historians might urge us to study others' successes and failures, and learn from those. Of course, none of this will help us grow or learn, if we are too busy, too sure of our self, or maybe too skeptical to consider looking for learning opportunities? What is your attitude? It has a lot to say about your ability and willingness to grow.

These one-liners about growth require no explanation:

THE BEST WAY TO LEARN SOMETHING IS TO TEACH IT TO SOMEONE ELSE

BY THE TIME I FIGURED OUT THE ANSWER, SOMEONE CHANGED THE QUESTION

YOU MAY HAVE TO FIGHT A BATTLE MORE THAN ONCE TO WIN IT
Margaret Thatcher

WHEN THE PUPIL IS READY, THE TEACHER WILL APPEAR
Buddha

IF YOU INVEST ENOUGH TIME AND STUDY IN ANY TOPIC, YOU WILL BECOME AN EXPERT

CAUTION...... I HAVE ALREADY MADE UP MY MIND, SO DON'T CONFUSE ME WITH THE FACTS
Like a quote by Roy Durstine

CHAPTER 11

STRESS/COPING

COPING WITH STRESS IS ESSENTIAL

When we are battered by stress (rain), having no way to cope leaves us vulnerable and hurting. But, if we have any way to cope (umbrella), we are able to function and feel more relaxed and competent. Just having stress is not automatically a problem, but if we are unable to muster coping strategies, then there is a problem

HOW DOES STRESS SHOW UP IN YOU?

Technically, stress is the way each of us is effected by pressure from the outside (and sometimes from inside); this pressure is referred to as stressors. So, how do you know you have stress? The specific ways stress shows up in us may be different from one person to the next, or from one time to another. Or, our stress may look a whole lot like that of our parents, maybe because we inherited it or learned it from them. My belief is stress can show up emotionally, mentally, physically, or spiritually. Emotionally, this stress may be worry, fear, anxiety, or depression (see next paragraph). Mentally, we may become forgetful, have difficulty solving problems, struggle to concentrate, or feel foggy. Physically, stress may appear as pain,

139

weakness, stomach aches, back strain, headaches, or exhaustion. Spiritually, we may experience new doubts, feel angry with God, or question if spiritually even exists. The more we realize the symptoms of stress, the more we are able to decide when we are in the need of stress relievers.

A CERTAIN LEVEL OF STRESS IS NECESSARY; BUT TOO MUCH CAN BE HARMFUL, EVEN DEADLY

I am reminded of a marionette when I think about needing a certain level of "stress" to function. When the strings of the marionette are slack, the puppet lays in a hump. Similarly, our muscles hold us up by being at the right level of tension. Some keep our legs straight and our feet at the right angle to stand. Without that basic amount of tension, our bodies could not function properly. At the same time, too much tension interferes with the body's functioning.

This is also true with our emotional balance. Too little stress in our lives stops us from functioning, and might involve some form of depression. Too much stress interferes with our functioning just as much and so is equally problematic. This condition of too much stress often involves anxiety, panic, obsessive-compulsive disorder, or post-traumatic stress disorder. Learning to manage our stress and keep it within a comfortable range is a valuable skill. Maintaining this workable level when major changes occur in our lives is an even greater challenge, and requires even more skill. Hopefully, many ideas in this book will help anyone wrestling with this essential life task. Happy reading.

THE STRESS PARADOX

Simply stated, I believe the paradox about stress is: when you need time to cope with stress the most – like during times with many changes and much pressure – this is precisely when you **don't have time** to do those things that would help you cope. That's right, we are too busy to take time to cope. I held a relaxation group a number of years ago, and at the end, one man remarked, "Wow, that was great. I wish I had time to do it every day." Later, I realized he was an accountant, and it was mid-February: tax season. He believed he did not have time to spend doing relaxation, but unfortunately he suffered for this belief. For others, rushing to catch a plane, or hurrying to the hospital, or running children all over town for their practices may seriously hamper their chance to utilize good coping tools - there is not enough time. Unless we realize the importance of coping and <u>insist</u> on taking the time, we are likely to remain stressed.

STRESS PARADOX -- NUMBER TWO

There is an old belief if you put a frog into a pot of hot water, the frog will jump right out. But, if you put the frog in a pot of cool water and slowly heat it up, the frog will cook and die. The point of the story is when we human beings are **exposed slowly to increasing stress**, we may not get out before it "cooks" us. We may end up with a serious mental disorder needing hospitalization or strong medications, or worse end in suicide. In contrast, if the stress appeared quickly and was immediately "too much," probably all of us would bail out quickly, and survive.

Recently, a woman whom I had seen in marriage counseling called me, very upset. Her husband finally said he was finished with the relationship. He had endured her criticism and belittling of him and the children for many years. It had taken him a long time for the water to reach the boiling point. Once he recognized the stress was "cooking" him (interesting analogy, he was a chef), he knew he needed out. For the wife, it was a total surprise - the water got hot instantly - and she quickly realized it "was really bad." She vowed to change, but it was too late for the husband. Oddly, even with this new awareness and ultimatum, she was unable to make the necessary changes.

TIRED, HUNGRY, LONELY, AND ANGRY -- BAD COMBINATION

AA has cautioned, for many years, all of us are more vulnerable to problems when we are "tired, hungry, lonely, or angry." These states set us up for emotional weakness. Then as a result, we show poor coping (drinking, eating, aggression, spending, drugs, depression, or self-aggression). Oddly, these states also set us up for physical problems, such as seizures, migraines, asthma, irritable bowel, and arthritic flare ups. The best advice - which we have all known for years - is to recognize these **weakened states** early, then quickly find ways to reduce or eliminate them. Don't let them wreak emotional or physical havoc.

WHY DO I OVERFLOW SO EASILY?

Here's another perspective to explain why we seem to get overwhelmed with stress "so easily." Usually, we attribute the intensity of our stress reactions to the size of the problem in front of us at that exact moment. But, there is another important factor: how "full up" were you before the latest problem even came along? Consider this analogy: if you pour *half* a glass of water into a glass *one-fourth full*, nothing bad happens. But, if you pour that same half glass of water into another that is *three-fourths full*, water goes everywhere. Definitely, the same is true for each of us: if we are **already mostly full** of stress or tension or worry, any **new stress can put us over the top**. We can easily "overflow" or "lose it." Unfortunately, many of us **do not realize how full** we are at any given moment, so we cannot predict how we will react to the next stressor, nor can we prevent the occurrence of a bad reaction.

There is a classic story in which a man arrives home from work at the end of his day and kicks the dog (who is blocking his way, laying in the middle of the hallway). Most of us immediately have sympathy for the dog - he did nothing to deserve being kicked. When we start looking for the problem, we realize it had to do with **how full** or stressed out the man was before he got home. If we were to retrace his last several hours, we would likely discover his boss criticized his latest project, he had to stay overtime for a customer's phone call, traffic was especially heavy, his engine light came on again, and the family left for the movie without him. That's how full he was, before he encountered the dog. "Full up," unaware, and the proverbial "one last thing" - he did not have a chance.

STRESS ILLUSTRATED

Picture this if you can. I once saw a cartoon showing a woman with huge, bloodshot eyes, straining neck, gritted teeth, and hair sticking straight out. The caption said: "I have one nerve left, and you are beginning to get on it." Great picture.

WHAT IS YOUR "STRAW THAT BROKE THE CAMEL'S BACK"?

This old expression gives me a powerful image of a camel loaded with straw. One piece of straw weighs almost nothing, so how can one straw break a camel's back? Clearly the answer must be the thousands of straws already on the camel, much like the glass of water we discussed previously (already quite full). **We are like the glass and the camel.**

Some people come to me complaining they are tired, depressed, or unable to get themselves going. They claim "nothing is going on," however. Yet, as I explore more about their life, numerous "straws" begin to appear. These **straws** make it clear they are burdened down with so much **weight,** which is clearly the cause of their inability to function. Sometimes, they are already **broken.** They have a mental breakdown, or a serious physical (or other mental) issue. When they recognize and admit all that is **piled on**, it can become both a source of relief and a key to their healing. An honest awareness of ourselves – for them and for us - can be difficult, because we are told: "Do not make mountains out of molehills," "Don't be dramatic," and "Don't overreact." To the surprise of these clients, I can help them realize – maybe for the first time – some of the "mountains" (or straws) are real and cause the stress.

GOOD SELF-ESTEEM, COPING SKILLS, AND SUPPORT GROUPS EASE STRESS

I attended a stress seminar where the speaker explained that, while she personally had much going on in her life putting pressure on her, she was handling it well. She attributed this to having strengths which offset the stressors: a positive self-esteem, a wide variety of coping skills, and family and friends supporting her. She strongly believed these strengths **made the difference for her**, and could also be used by others to manage their stress better, too.

So what exactly are these **offsetting strengths**? She provided many examples of her coping skills, which involved activities like walking, writing, beating a rug with a broom, allowing tears, and yoga. She identified a support network (grief groups, sewing circles, Bible study, college classes, and family members). She admitted self-esteem was harder to quantify, but she offered ideas such as giving herself credit for successes, realizing her positive traits and abilities, and accepting "thanks" for help she provided to others. When those aspects of her stress puzzle were strong, outside pressure definitely had less effect on her; and we can do the same.

THE BEST COPING SKILLS ARE ALL QUITE CHILDISH.

Since stress is a normal part of life, I believe one of our responsibilities is to find ways to cope successfully with it. But, much of our training emphasizes being mature, rational, and "intellectual." In contrast, my own experience shows me the best, most helpful coping skills are **quite childish** - often involving a blatant, unbridled display of emotion. For example, one client stated when she got angry with someone, she took a walk around the block, putting each foot on the face of that person with every step. Childish? yes, but effective. Crying is another childish but valuable coping tool. Since it is often considered inappropriate or unsophisticated, many of us avoid it.

One important guideline for coping strategies is: it is *not* ok to hurt yourself or someone else. No hitting, cutting, speeding, fighting, etc. So, what do these childish strategies look like? Well, if you are afraid, it may be helpful to ask someone you trust to simply hold you...then shake and/or cry all you want. If you feel lonely, cry, and then push yourself to go to a restaurant or library where there are other people and hang out. If you are angry, hit the bed with a tennis racket (watch the light fixture). With each of these, you inflict no harm to yourself or to anyone else. Also, each one is childish, but each will help deal with stress.

During another group, one person volunteered he used a "worry tree." He explained that, on his way home from work each day, he "hung" his job stress and worries on a big tree overhanging his route. The next day, he picked up those worries on his way back to work - but never took them home. Silly (childish), huh?

EVEN "BAD" COPING STRATEGIES REDUCE STRESS

Fortunately, there are many different coping strategies we can use to handle stress. Yet, some of those strategies have very definite, negative side effects, and I consider them to be **bad coping strategies**. What might be confusing is how a "bad" strategy can be helpful: well, they reduce stress. Consider drinking: while drinking, most people are less anxious or worried, and less upset about any current situation. But, the side effects - later - to drinking are clear: hangovers, money lost, angering the family, wrecks from drunk driving, liver disease, and missed work days. Similarly, gambling makes people feel better during the challenge and the excitement; but, again it brings problems, later: lost money, the need to gamble more and more to feel good, upset family members, and the need to sneak around.

Other "bad" coping strategies include having an affair, using drugs, overspending, fast driving, overeating, and aggression. For each of these, there is definitely some stress relief while doing them, for sure; but, there are serious negative consequences afterward.

THE LONGEST JOURNEY BEGINS WITH THE FIRST STEP
Like a quote by Lao Tzu

I hope the truth of this one-liner is obvious. When we focus on the "whole mess," we can be easily discouraged, never starting, and feeling defeated. Rather than getting "stressed out" and stalled by being overwhelmed – "I don't know how to fix it," "Where do I start?" "What if I fail?" – it helps to look only for the first step, and take it. Many of us might never start a new project (or job, relationship, career, a major vacation), unless we can decide to **take the first step**. Most likely, that will lead us to the next step or even to other people who can help us learn to cope. Planning ahead is a great help, but there are times when this is not possible. For those times, we can decide to start, take the risk, and see what happens. "I know it is a risk, but I am talking about taking *one* step."

YOU WANT ME TO SURVIVE?
THEN, DON'T TAKE AWAY MY "ONLY" COPING SKILL

Often, we, and others close to us, do not realize we have become dependent on only one coping method, and we have come to rely on it greatly. If it is taken away for any reason, we essentially have no coping skills left. A common example is alcohol. When someone stops drinking "cold turkey," they often end up with no coping skill in place of the drinking. As soon as they experience stress, they may go right back to their **familiar coping skill** - drinking. Some people are able to connect with AA, so, at least they have something positive, a support group always available. Developing other coping skills is important to their success with stopping alcohol. Smoking can involve the same problems, with the same results. Similarly, stopping other addictions can also eliminate a person's only coping strategy, as in shoplifting or eating. What if someone wants to stop, but they have no new coping skill to use? If they anticipate this problem and plan alternative methods *before* ceasing the addictive behavior (or soon after), they have a chance at success. For many people, a support group may be their first choice. I also suggest watching what other people do and borrowing what works for them. It may also help to remind ourselves those "bad" coping strategies did not work, in the long run.

PEOPLE ARE A LOT LIKE BALLOONS

Do you remember as a child playing with balloons? If you blew the balloon up just a little, you could squeeze it, smash it down almost flat, and pinch it in the middle to make two bubbles. But, if you blew it up more, you had to be careful, because being rough with it would make it pop. If you blew it up even more, you had to be extremely careful, since even brushing it on a smooth surface might pop it. Fortunately, letting some air out made the balloon pliable again.

Stress does the same thing to people. When we have a little stress in our lives or are carrying a little strain around with us, we are flexible and can cope with bumps and outside pressure. But, as we fill up more with tension and stress, we "pop" more easily and our coping declines greatly. Then, if we take on even more stress, almost anything can set us off, even the smallest demand, or change, or challenge. Luckily, like the balloon, if we **let off some pressure before we blow**, we are again more flexible and able to cope. The trick is to **notice when we are full up**, or better yet when we are beginning to fill up, so we can use our stress management tools to take off some of the pressure before there is a problem. Then we can be flexible again…like the balloon.

THERE IS NO WAY TO COMPLETELY AVOID CONFLICTS WITH OTHERS; THE TRICK IS TO RECOVER QUICKLY

This idea was presented earlier, but this time I will focus more on stress. Conflict in relationships can be a major source of stress. This is especially true if a problem drags on and on, with no resolution. Each person may feel the need - and responsibility - to check on it occasionally, which most likely renews their stress. Worse yet, some couples are unable to resolve any issues, leaving a backlog of unresolved problems, an easy source of additional "fuel." While some of this cannot be avoided, it surely can be minimized. When problems are resolved quickly, stress for both people, and for their relationship, automatically lessens.

Recovering quickly requires a willingness to talk, respect, compromise, budge a little, and honor the other person and the relationship as worth approaching peacefully. If this is not where both people are, they might do well to consider whether to even stay in the relationship. If both are interested in lowering their stress and finding more peace at home, tools to help them are available (some even in this book). Any work involved pays off with reduced stress for both.

HUMAN BEINGS NEED TO DECOMPRESS— AND NOT JUST FROM SCUBA DIVES

The idea of decompression is important in the sport of scuba diving. If someone does not follow a strict set of procedures after a deep dive, they will most likely experience serious medical problems. Well, many people suffer from daily "deep dives into the stress pool," but they rarely get any kind of "decompression." What they need is time to slow down, unwind, and let go of the day's pressure, especially after a hard day at work or a difficult family event. When they don't take time for stress management, they are likely to be irritable, grouchy, sullen, physically tired, or worse, physically ill. **Emotional decompression** can be a walk, reading, a hobby, fun cooking, a quiet drive, a hike, sitting beside the water, writing, kicking the dirt, etc. We all need time to decompress

PEOPLE CAN BE A LOT LIKE SUPER-SATURATED SOLUTIONS

In a college chemistry class, I was introduced to the phenomenon of **super-saturated solutions**. We were instructed to dissolve sugar in a beaker of water, and then slowly add more sugar until we had to really stir to get it all to dissolve. In examining the beaker, the water was completely clear. Then we were instructed to scratch the inside of the beaker with our glass stirring rod. Well, sugar quickly sank to the bottom. If we stirred hard again, the sugar disappeared, again. Then, with a simple scratch of the stirring rod, some sugar once more dropped to the bottom. Interesting, eh?

I am convinced the same phenomenon occurs with people - we can **get too full** and hold more than we can and still be **stable**. At those times, we are barely able to hold all the stress, tension, pressure, and challenges, but we keep going and looking good. (Remember the clear water.) Then some little "scratch" **disrupts the balance** we were holding so precariously, and we lose it. The scratch may be as simple as a baby crying, traffic, a political ad, or a sudden noise - just enough to disrupt our **tentative equilibrium**.

Grief can be that way. People may contain their feelings quite well until a particular song, a familiar-sounding voice, or an oft-visited restaurant comes on to the radar. Since many people try to keep their feelings in check, there can be a build-up of "stuffed" emotions. The balance is maintained, until some little thing disrupts it. Then, all the sugar goes to the bottom: the grief feelings pour out like a flood, surprising other people around, but surprising the one who was super-saturated, too.

VICIOUS CYCLES CAN BE STOPPED ANYWHERE ALONG THE CYCLE

Many of the problems people face with stress become vicious cycles. For example, a person who has much anxiety at work may have difficulty concentrating. They make mistakes or fall behind on assigned tasks, and become even more anxious – starting the cycle over again. To break this pattern, most people are likely to think they "just have to" stop being anxious. But, if they ask for assistance to get caught up, or if some responsibilities are reassigned, either of those can break the cycle, too. They can also use a variety of ways to reduce their anxiety (perhaps slowed breathing or relaxation), which does break the cycle.

An accountant was referred to me by his doctor due to stress and anxiety. He was also ordered to take a medical leave from work, for two months. His typical work day included arriving early to get a head start, working through breaks and lunch because he was "in the middle of something," leaving late (after trying to "get caught up"), and taking work home with him. I strongly encouraged him, when he returned to work, to get up at each break and at lunch. I asked him to walk to the farthest corner of the building ... slowly ... without any detours. This was especially helpful since he got to relax at least three times a day, and his anxiety did not have a chance to build for hours. He believed he had to work extra hard because he did not have a college degree. We discovered, while he was on leave, it took *two* people to replace him – and one was a CPA! Fortunately, when he returned to his job, he improved his situation three ways: by breaking the physical tension cycle each day, by using deep breathing, and by drastically altering his expectations and self-judgment.

LOOKING FOR CLOSURE -- "WHAT IF . . ." MAY HELP

In some situations, not knowing what happened, who was responsible, why it happened, or how it ended can be disturbing - and stressful. Often, the answers are not available anywhere, from anyone. One way to handle or cope with such unknowns may be accept that answers may never be found, and our best option is to let go and move on.

For some, they need more. For them, the need to understand is too strong. While there may be no way to accurately and officially understand, asking some "what if" questions may still help. For example, if a friend committed suicide, for no apparent reason, then asking ourselves "What if they had more going on than we realized?" or "What if an old medical problem resurfaced?" or "What if I did not know them as well as I thought?" or "What if they tried to present only an optimistic side to all of us?" or "What if the intensity of their pain and suffering broke through, despite their best efforts?" Simply considering such questions may put a new perspective on our thinking and help us cope.

If I do not **understand myself**, some of the same questions may help. I might ask, "What if some childhood hurt is no longer safely stuffed?" or "What if a recent song/ movie/ picture/ stranger triggered an old memory?" or "What if some part of me knows I need to deal with some hidden issue to continue to grow?" In some cases, our best guesses may help us move on and not stay stuck, which amounts to less stress and better coping.

Obviously, asking thought-provoking questions is an important part of this exercise. It is also important to spend time answering the questions, without becoming judgmental and without obsessing. In working on the questions, we may benefit from having a trusted friend provide their ideas, too. It might also help to do some writing, put it away for a time, and then return to review it or add to it later. After a reasonable time of asking and answering, the last step is choosing a way of understanding that allows you to put the situation to rest.

Chapter 12

PROBLEM SOLVING

SERENITY PRAYER

God grant me the strength to change the things I can,
The serenity to accept the things I cannot change,
And the wisdom to know the difference.
Reinhold Niebuhr

PROBLEMS CANNOT BE SOLVED AT THE SAME LEVEL OF THINKING THAT CREATED THEM.
Albert Einstein

We have all heard the saying "Two heads are better than one." I think these two sayings are promoting a new and improved degree of wisdom in order to solve a problem we created. Continuing to look at a problem or trying to address a problem in the same way we did when the problem first occurred, seldom works to produce a solution. What may be required is to look from a new perspective, get advice from someone else, or let the solution come to us during our sleep. Or, we may need to write it down, make a diagram of it, or talk it through with another person - or with the dog! Each of these can offer a special opportunity to utilize a new level of thinking . . . and a new way to find a good solution.

MOST OF THE TIME, THERE IS NO RIGHT ANSWER

In our society, we place great emphasis on being right and finding the right answer to every problem. At times, this can lead to heated and hurtful arguments that negatively affect relationships. Our push for perfectionism can cause us great suffering over the need to find the right answer, or our need to win. What seems more helpful is to accept there are numerous "good" answers to most problems, but rarely any perfect solutions. And, there are some problems where there is simply no right answer at all. With that in mind, we can stop arguing, stop insisting on our way, or stop struggling and get on with the issue of selecting and implementing a **workable solution.**

EVERY DECISION I EVER MADE WAS THE BEST I COULD DO AT THE TIME
Jon Connelly

Many of us doubt ourselves before, during, and especially after we make a decision. We often re-think and second-guess ourselves. Later, based on new information or poor results from our decision, we may even question our sanity. But, if we look carefully at the process we went through with any decision, we would realize **we weighed the options (maybe briefly), selected the option making the most sense, and then took action - every single time.** In truth, we selected the option that looked best at the time, even when we realized our option may have held some risk. We definitely **can give ourselves credit** for a good decision, because we chose the best option at the time we had to make the decision. Even if it did not work out well later on, we could not have known that when we had to make the decision. Furthermore, there were many times we chose the **only decision we could** at the time.

Again, an example may help. Teenage boys on Main Street on Saturday night might propose buying a case of beer and heading out west of town to party. It seems mostly ok, since surely no one will ever know. One teen realizes the pros and cons, even the seemingly-slim possibility of being caught, but decides to go, because the chance to "bond" with his friends is the most important part of this decision. Later, when the red, flashing lights are headed their way, the decision does not look so good. But, *before that reality hit - after* he made his decision – I believe he did the best he could, based on what was important to him at the time.

IT'S NOT ONLY IMPORTANT TO MAKE A GOOD DECISION, BUT ALSO TO MAKE A DECISION GOOD.

Let's look at this decision thing further. When most of us make an important decision, we do our "homework" fairly well, *before* we decide anything, as just mentioned. But what **we often fail to do is fully support ourselves and the decision** *after* **it is made.** Dangerously, we re-hash, question our own thinking, ask "but, what if," guess how much better the alternatives would have worked, and basically undermine the decision and <u>our</u> whole decision process. In turn, we **lose confidence** in our decision and in ourselves, and then the decision often begins to fail; it fails at least partly due to this new skeptical, self-fulfilling prophesy. Instead of allowing this to happen, we would all benefit greatly from **reassuring ourselves and supporting our decision**, so the decision (and we) stays strong. Later, if I decide a decision is not working, it is ok to change it. Even then, it is *not* ok to criticize my original decision as "wrong." I learned something from my choice. I did the best I could at the time. No "buts."

PROBLEMS AND DILEMMAS ARE DIFFERENT: ONE CAN BE FIXED, THE OTHER CANNOT

Getting confused about "solving" problems and dilemmas seems quite easy to do. By nature, problems have solutions (maybe several) and once a solution is applied, the problem is taken care of, resolved, or fixed. But, dilemmas do not have "solutions" as such. Instead of solutions, there are options to make the situation better, but **not** fix or resolve it fully. The options do allow us to handle the dilemma, in one way or another, and move on, but not fix it.

For example, a flat tire on your car is a problem. This problem can be fixed temporarily by replacing it with the spare, then permanently by patching the tire or buying a new one. In contrast, having an old car or a trouble-prone new car does not have a simple or clear solution. You can put money into it as needed and presumably keep it running for an extended period of time. Or, as another option, but not a solution, you can trade it in. This likely means time spent shopping, loss of investment (in the new car), higher insurance, new car payments, new fears about others' doors being slammed into it, etc. Deciding to keep it or sell it offers two options, but since both bring new issues, neither "solves or fixes" this dilemma.

What is especially tricky is mistakenly calling dilemmas "problems;" this implies we can reasonably expect that, when we finish, the dilemmas are solved. But, as already noted, dilemmas cannot be solved or fixed. An example of mislabeling a dilemma as a problem might be when our son or daughter has difficulty in public school; the simple solution is to change to a private school. But, neither of the two options guarantees to fix all aspects of this dilemma. While public school is free, special academic services are mandated, and our child's friends are there, public school also involves large classes, long lines at the bathroom/lunch room, more kids who experience problems with school, and overworked teachers. Private schools usually have no transportation, higher academic requirements, and a sizable cost, while offering smaller classes, more kids who are ready to learn, teachers who may be more motivated, and more parent involvement. Whichever you choose, you gain some and lose some; so this dilemma is "dealt with," but in no way is it a problem that can simply be fixed.

HAVING OPTIONS HELPS, EVEN IF WE DO NOT USE THEM

So often I hear people say they have no options - there is nothing they can think of to handle a problem or dilemma. At other times, people say they are stuck with only one way (option) to resolve a situation, and they do not like the solution. I believe we all benefit by finding more options when we find ourselves in such a frustrating spot. Generating options can give us a morale boost in these situations; and this can often be done by asking others, brainstorming, or noticing what others have done before us. In turn, having multiple options makes our choice much easier. This may have something to do with our desire to have control over situations (which is missing when there are "no" or "only one" option available). There may be a bit of a paradox in this, too: we feel better having more than one option, even if in the end, we "choose" the only one we had at the beginning.

PERSISTENCE OFTEN PAYS OFF

As the story goes, a circus came to town and boasted they had a strong man who could not be pulled off a pole by any team of horses. On a designated day, all the local farmers showed up with their teams. One by one, they hooked up to the strong man's harness and tried to break his grip on the pole. One by one they jerked against the harness, backed up and jerked again, but failed. Then, the last farmer brought his two scrawny mules to the front. Everyone laughed while he confidently hooked up his team. The two mules walked slowly forward to tighten the rope, and then they leaned into their harnesses - and waited. Soon, the strong man's grip began to loosen and gradually the mules pulled him off the pole. Sometimes, to solve a problem, you just have to hang in there and wait - and stop being a "jerk."

BRAINSTORMING IS A GREAT TOOL WHEN WE GET STUCK

When we are looking for a solution to a problem, there is a tendency to be immediately critical of the ideas offered. Unfortunately, people become uncomfortable with the process, and this quickly stops the flow of ideas. Our chance to solve the problem becomes much less likely. When this happens, we find it easy to give up and walk away, disgusted and stumped. But, brainstorming can be a big help to turn this stalled situation around.

I was taught four **steps to solve problems using brainstorming**: (1) carefully define the problem, making sure not to tackle several problems at once, (2) brainstorm – gather as many ideas as possible, while requiring "no criticism," "anything goes," and "the more the better," (3) evaluate each idea, keeping the list open ended and combining thoughts where useful, (4) try one idea to see how it works. Then, any or all of the steps can be repeated if necessary.

Once, a young woman came to me saying she could not sleep. To be clear about the nature of this problem, I asked what she thought caused it. She was sure it was because she was afraid her ex-boyfriend was still upset with her, and might break in at night to harm her. We brainstormed, and the stream of ideas went like this: move to another town, change your name and move across town, get a roommate, get a guard dog, hire a body guard, hire a hit man, shoot him yourself, get a big boyfriend, or marry someone.

155

When I first suggested the "shoot him" idea, she did not want to write it down, but I insisted - that is how brainstorming works best: anything goes. When we did the evaluation step, I adjusted the "shoot him" idea to her possibly shooting him with "mace." She smiled right away and was sure she could; she even seemed excited about the idea. For $5, she bought mace (pepper spray), put it under her pillow, and began sleeping great.

RATING PROS AND CONS CAN CLARIFY A HARD CHOICE

Most of us know how listing pros and cons provides clarification when we are trying to solve a difficult problem or make a difficult decision. A trick to enhance this idea (of just listing pros and cons) is to rate each pro and each con on a simple three-point scale, giving a "3" to those most important positives or negatives, a "2" to medium ones, and a "1" to the least important. When these are added together, the totals can bring surprising clarity to a seemingly split decision.

Back in my 20s, I was offered a part-time job that looked good, but required staying away from my family one night a week. I wrote my list of pros and cons, re-worked the list, talked to others, even put it away for 24 hours, but I was still stumped. When I finally rated each item on my list, the total was "19" pros and "24" cons. I caught myself saying, "I knew that," but I really did not. The numbers definitely clarified how much each item meant to me.

EMOTIONAL DECISIONS ARE DANGEROUS

We live in an intellectual culture, and the culture demands we make decisions on a rational – not emotional – basis. I agree in part: make no decisions *totally based* on emotions. But, in the big picture, we are both **emotional and intellectual** beings; the best decisions would seem to be the ones **respecting both aspects** of who we are. Purely emotional responses can cause difficulty, as can totally intellectual ones; still, our society seems more accepting of rational/intellectual decisions. For my part, I believe some combination is best. We would also benefit from including a third aspect of ourselves - our intuition - which is valuable and usually quite accurate. It is sometimes called "the quiet voice of reason." Respecting each part of who we are results in the best decisions.

IF YOU HAVE TO EAT A BUCKET OF FROGS, EAT THE BIGGEST ONE FIRST
Mark Twain

Hopefully, none of us have to eat any frogs, but there are many difficult things people do have to do. It definitely helps to take on the hardest part first. Then, everything else is easier. The worst is over and "it's all downhill from there." For example, when asking for family forgiveness, talking first to the person who was hurt the most may make apologizing to the others a bit easier. Clearly, packing suitcases into the trunk of the car may be easier if the big cases are placed first. Or, if you plan to paint the whole house, painting the largest or most difficult room first would make lots of sense. On a much harder level, announcing you and your partner are getting a divorce may work best if the one who will struggle the most with the information is told first - telling the others will then be easier.

This idea is true for many problems, in the family, with neighbors, and at work or school. But, most of us tend to work the opposite way, taking on the easier parts of a job first. Generally, this leaves us with increasing levels of stress as we complete the increasingly-more-difficult aspects of the task. At times, it may be best to handle some situations in this "opposite" way. For example, if a person wants to announce to family and friends about being gay, telling the easiest or most-trusted person first may create a base of support and make telling the others easier. Swallowing the big frog first may work in many situations, but not all.

TRY ASSERTIVE SKILLS TO SOLVE PEOPLE PROBLEMS

I have identified assertive training as a rich source of skills to handle various situations. The **broken record** technique was described and illustrated earlier. There are other ideas to help us get what we want when we are faced with a difficult person. One is to **agree in principle**, which involves not arguing with another person, but vaguely or theoretically going along with an accusation or negative statement they made: "You are the angriest person I know" gets a response of "I do get angry at times, don't I?" By "agreeing" in this way, it is possible to take the fight out of their statement and "the wind out of their sails."

Another skill is called **negative inquiry**. This involves asking the other person to "tell me more" about my faults and problems; maybe asking them several times to elaborate. Without agreeing, disagreeing, or apologizing, you can solicit their clarification until they are unable to think of anything more to add. Again, *not disagreeing* takes much of the fight out of the other person and their complaint, making it easier to solve a problem - or get away.

There are a number of other such skills, and I recommend them for solving problems involving other people. Remember, the goal of assertiveness is to do what I can to get what I want, without hurting another person or myself...and without giving up.

CHAPTER 13

FOR THERAPISTS -- MOSTLY

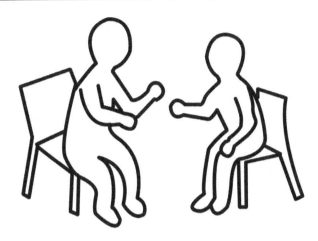

THE PERSON I AM HELPING HAS THE ANSWERS ALREADY

This is a valuable perspective for a therapist to have. As much as we may want to demonstrate our extensive training or our amazing skills as a therapist, the patient ultimately has to "find" the answers that work best for them and their situation. Our job is to guide, suggest, or encourage them to think in new ways which more easily reveal answers. Most therapists enjoy sharing/teaching information that may help someone learn new perspectives (making discovery easier). Still, the client is clearly in charge of incorporating that information, finding their unique way to make it work for them, and developing confidence about applying it in the future. When they do, they may well understand they have *other* answers already, too.

THERE ARE NO PSYCHIATRIC EMERGENCIES.

Long ago, a psychiatrist whom I respected emphatically stated this: there are no emergencies in mental health. I was surprised, but eager to understand. He explained a drug overdose is a medical emergency. Someone standing on a bridge threatening to jump is a police emergency, as is any other suicidal threat (because suicide is illegal in most states). Someone who is depressed is not an emergency at all, since this depression has likely been going on for some time. Someone who is hallucinating may be inappropriate and uncomfortable to others, but again is not causing an emergency. Anyone who threatens others – even if clearly paranoid – must be handled first by the police. Interesting perspective, I think.

A RED LIGHT MEANS "GO"

I heard this powerful instruction at a workshop years ago, and it has been quite helpful for me since. When someone shows hesitation or resistance to an idea, it likely means there is an important problem, struggle, or set of feelings connected with it. Their reluctance is the **red light,** and the likely value in pursuing this subject with this client is the **go.** (This incorporates another valuable therapy strategy - to listen and notice inconsistencies.) Urging the client to "go" also gives credibility to an issue they may have pushed down and ignored for years. Unfortunately, people seem inclined to ignore bad memories and past hurts, even when it may be valuable for them to address these.

SYMPATHIZING OR EMPATHIZING CAN BE "POISONOUS"
Jon Connelly

Most therapists are taught it is good to empathize with a client. This helps *validate* feelings, and begins the process of working through them. This is supposed to be one of the best ways we can help others as a therapist. For some therapists, this involves asking clients to relive old memories and re-experience old hurts, as the only way to work through and release those feelings.

A different approach offers a hopefully less painful and more beneficial way to work through those old hurts. This idea is based on knowing that, since those hurts are from **past events that are over**, it is time for the feelings to be over, too. While a certain feeling may have been appropriate at the time, that **event is not going on** *now* **- and neither should the feeling.** The hurtful event is in the past, and that is where the pain belongs, too. Any feelings are over, done, finished, gone.

Unfortunately, our sympathy with our clients' feelings may affirm that having those feelings *today* is somehow correct - our sympathy validates the feeling as it happens *now*. We may also give the impression clients must experience the feelings *now,* to correctly handle and eventually eliminate them. In contrast, if this same situation occurred at home with a family member who became emotionally upset remembering a past event, we would likely urge them to calm down and to realize this is "now," the memory was "then." For example, if a family member began feeling strong fear as they described a bear encounter at Yellowstone some months before, while sitting in our living room, we would likely bring them back to reality and help them calm down, ie, "You are not at Yellowstone, now." Maybe we should consider doing the same with our clients.

"NORMALIZING" IS A POWERFUL TOOL

Many of my clients have expressed a belief their reactions – and especially their feelings – are ridiculous, totally unusual, and weird. Of course, they think that makes them weird, too. I believe helping them see their responses are much like anyone might have in the same situation and therefore *are not unusual*. In other words, their responses were "normal." One way to do this is to tell stories of others and how they reacted in similar situations. I believe it helps them greatly to know they are not bizarre or "crazy," in their behavior, feelings, or thinking.

IF THE THERAPIST IS WORKING HARDER THAN THE CLIENT, SOMETHING IS WRONG

At times, I find myself working hard to make a point, bolster self-esteem, or help a person understand a key concept in therapy; then I catch myself. My effort is out of proportion to their effort, which will never work. There are brief times when a therapist may work hard to achieve a particular goal. But if this imbalance of effort happens often, or for a good length of time, something is wrong. Is the client not motivated to make changes? Is the therapist pushing too hard? Is there a distraction? Is the patient lost regarding the ideas being discussed? This is a good time to pause, and discuss the situation.

THERAPISTS SOMETIMES PLAY DETECTIVE

When new clients walk through my door, they are usually fairly clear about their basic concerns or major complaints. However, they are often vague about why they feel or behave the way they do, or what they think may be causing their problems. Some clarification is needed for me as their therapist to know how to proceed. How this clarification is achieved may depend on the orientation of the therapist, but in many ways, I think therapists end up being **detectives**. Identifying and piecing together clues, recognizing the many issues that all effect the person's emotions, and offering a summary explanation may not only provide the **directions for therapy**, but also a sense of calm by finally having an **understanding** of himself/herself. I believe this is one of the most powerful tools we therapists bring to the art of helping others.

One of the common difficulties I believe amateur detectives have is to begin with an assumption there is **one major cause** for everyone's struggles. Most of my clients have been looking for just that, but have had little success finding *that one cause*, often leaving them frustrated. To the contrary, I believe there are usually multiple causes, not one. Part of my detective work involves *not* trying to simplify, so valuable information is not overlooked. When multiple causes can be identified, my clients are often surprised, but relieved they did not miss an easy answer. And, with multiple "causes," even if each one seems to have a very small effect on the problem, clients get to appreciate the whole picture, ie, that all those "causes" added up together can explain their struggle.

SO, WHAT IS A REASONABLE PUNISHMENT FOR YOU?

Sometimes, people hold on to a past behavior (a "sin," a hurt toward another, a major mistake, or a terrible oversight), and suffer because of it. While others looking on from the outside would likely believe it is time for them to accept forgiveness and move on, there often is a stumbling block: the person is **not ready to forgive himself/herself**. In exploring this, they often seem to be holding on to the idea they have not been punished enough, yet. I have found it helpful to explore how much retribution they believe would be reasonable. Typically, they have no idea, so I start with a "sentence" of 100 years; so far, no one has seen that as reasonable, and I certainly am glad. Next, I work my way down: 50 years? 10 years? Then, to some number of years that would make sense to them. Once a number is set, I help them see they have *most likely "served" more time than that, already*. Maybe it is **time to be finished with the punishment**. Maybe it is time for them to let go of the past "sin," embrace forgiveness, and make plans in line with their new freedom.

PEOPLE MAY NEED TO HEAR THE SAME MESSAGE SEVERAL TIMES

One frustration I experience is hearing a client praise an uncle (brother/mother/neighbor) for helpful advice. Why frustrating? Because I have gone over the same idea with them, perhaps several times. But, apparently it did not stick when they were with me. I have decided many of us, including me, need to hear an idea several times before it sinks in. And, who knows, the barber may get credit.

SOMETIMES IT HELPS TO TAKE A "THERAPY VACATION"

There are times, during therapy, when a brief recess or vacation may be helpful. This allows time to practice or mull over ideas. Perhaps, then, the client will be in a better place of understanding. During this time, clients can renew their energy or desire to work hard again in therapy. I have also observed a supervisor using this with clients who were not "ready" for therapy, along with a suggestion to return when they are ready to work hard.

SOME CLIENTS JUST NEED A THERAPY "BOOSTER SHOT"

I assume medical doctors still give "booster shots" for tetanus or other common illnesses. When clients achieve their goals with me, they may terminate in order to work on their mental health on their own. Many of them call, sometime later, to review the techniques we discussed or to refresh their memory about how they can better take care of themselves and their relationships. Generally, one or two sessions seem adequate to get them squarely back on track, and they terminate with me again. I consider this a psychotherapy booster shot.

SEX IS OFTEN A BAROMETER FOR THE REST OF THE MARITAL RELATIONSHIP

In working with couples, the quality of their sexual relationship is often indicative of how the rest of the relationship is working, or not. Therapists are sometimes hesitant to ask about such personal areas of the marriage, but this information can be helpful in many ways. Even how they talk about their sexual relationship may provide helpful information. Of course, there are exceptions to every rule, and there have been a few times in my work with troubled couples when they seemed to be held together mostly, or only, by a good sexual connection.

DON'T ASK QUESTIONS IF YOU DON'T WANT THE ANSWER

As therapists, we are trained to ask questions, rather than make statements or jump to conclusions. But, we have not always been taught to ask therapeutically relevant questions. Sometimes, when we get **curious**, we might ask offhandedly about salary, or well-known friends, or political preferences. Such questions may leave us with information we are unsure how to handle or these questions may be offensive to our client (and we got no benefit from asking it). Out of curiosity, we might ask what they liked or did not like about a previous therapist; but, this question should be a serious part of therapy or never asked at all.

IN A FAMILY SESSION, WE MAY TALK ABOUT YOU "IN FRONT OF YOUR BACK"

In my experience, teens are often reluctant to talk when the whole family is in my office. Since I consider this valuable time, if a teenager "clams up" and refuses to participate, I urge the rest of the family to talk about problems and even talk about *them* (the teenager) "in front of their back," rather than behind it! In most cases with a quiet teen, they soon cannot restrain themselves. They begin defending their actions, making comments, answering questions (rather than have someone answer for them), and eventually begin participating normally.

DON'T LISTEN TO THE NEXT THING I SAY

When I do sessions with couples, part of my focus is to help them see ways they add to their conflict and hurt with their communication. When one person makes what I believe is an un-workable comment, I call a "time out" and address that person directly. I help him/her re-work their last communication, replacing it with a constructive statement. During this re-work, I may ask the other partner "not to listen" to what we are saying - and not respond. My goal? Prevent a likely-negative reply to a clearly un-workable statement. I hope this serves as **modeling** for the couple, so they know what to do at home on their own. During the "time out," the other partner is encouraged to listen to the improved version, and then decide how to answer. Obviously, the quiet partner hears everything, and hopefully benefits from being aware of how to make positive communication changes.

FAMILY MEMBERS ARE ALL INTERCONNECTED

In a family therapy workshop I attended years ago, I clearly remember one of the demonstrations the presenter used. To help us understand how family members are connected to each other, he had about ten people form a circle up on the stage. He brought out a rope and handed the end to one person, then stretched it across the circle for another person to hold on, then back across to another person, and back-and-forth until he was out of rope. As you might guess, the rope formed a maze – with all the people connected – mimicking life.

Then, to demonstrate how families respond to change, he asked one person to take a step backward. He urged us to watch closely. When the man stepped back, he was quickly pulled back into the circle. What happened? The "family" rejected the one member making a move, and they quickly re-established the status quo by pulling him back in place. Next, the leader asked the person to take two steps back, and the presenter said he would help this "family member" step back. This time, when the one person stepped back the entire circle shuffled around, shifted, and re-set. Once again, we were all asked to describe what happened, and we got it, somewhat. The presenter provided an informative explanation - when one person changes, the whole family structure first tries to prevent it. It there is more pressure to change, the family is then forced to make many adjustments to establish a new balance. He emphasized no one can make changes without affecting others around them - others who are then confronted with making changes, too.

One more one-liner for therapists which requires no explanation:

DON'T TALK, DON'T TRUST, AND DON'T FEEL -- THE RULES FOR A DYSFUNCTIONAL FAMILY

METAPHORS

WHAT ARE YOU FEEDING -- IN YOURSELF?

A young Indian boy asked his grandfather why some braves in their tribe were kind and others were mean. His grandfather said their tribe believed inside every young brave lives a good wolf and a bad wolf, both trying to gain control over that brave. The boy thought a moment and asked his grandfather which wolf wins. The grandfather said simply, "The one you feed."

HOW LONG DO YOU DWELL ON NEGATIVE STUFF?

There is a story from long ago about two monks who were traveling. They came across a young woman who was beautifully dressed and standing beside a muddy ditch. It was obvious she wanted to get across, so one monk picked her up, carried her across the ditch, and went on his way. An hour later, the second monk remarked he was surprised the first monk picked up the woman. He reminded the first man of their vows to have no contact with people from the outside world; what was he thinking? The first monk calmly said, "I put that woman down an hour ago, but you are still carrying her."

GOOD OR BAD - HOW DO YOU DECIDE?

Long ago, a farmer was visiting his neighbor and mentioned that his mare had run away. The neighbor quickly said, "Oh, that's bad, really bad;" but the first farmer said, "Well, it could be bad or it could be good." Several weeks later, the two were visiting again, and the first farmer said, "My horse came back, with a colt at its side." The other farmer said, "Wow, that's good, really good;" but, again, the first farmer said, "It could be good or it could be bad." Later, they met again, and the first farmer mentioned that his son fell out of a tree and broke his arm. As before, the second farmer was quick to conclude, "That's bad, that's bad." But, the first farmer persisted, "It could be bad or it could be good." The next time they

167

met, the first farmer stated, "The army came by yesterday to recruit all the young men, but my son could not go because of his broken arm." The second farmer replied, "Well, that's really good." The first farmer maintained, "It could be good, or it could be bad." Like the neighbor most of us are quick to jump to conclusions, especially about what is bad in our lives. It may be best for all of us to wait, give it some time, and then see whether an event is actually "good or bad."

DOES THAT ANSWER YOUR QUESTION?

A ten-year-old boy approached his father and asked, "Where did I come from?" The father quickly decided it was time for his son to learn about the birds and the bees. They went in a quiet room, where dad explained all about babies, sex, sperm and eggs. . . the whole process. At the end, the father asked if that answered the boy's question. The boy said, "Well, Billy said he was from Detroit, and I wondered where I came from."

YOU COULD HAVE GOTTEN MORE OUT

There was a ten-year-old girl whose father was a minister. One Sunday, she accompanied him when he went as a guest preacher to a small, country church. Just inside the door was a basket in which people were putting money. She watched as her father added $5 as he passed it. He preached the service, and at the end one of the people there gave him all the money in the basket - it was all they had. The girl observed all of this and was quiet until half-way home. Then she observed, out loud, "Dad, if you had put more in, you'd have gotten more out." So... how much have you put in?

WHEN FILLING ANY JAR, PUT IN THE BIG ROCKS FIRST Or DON'T JUMP TO CONCLUSIONS

I saw a demonstration once in which the leader had a number of large rocks on the table and a large jar. He asked us all to watch as he "filled" the jar with the rocks. Then, he asked if it was truly full or not. Most everyone in the room quickly agreed it was completely full. Well, without saying anything, he brought out a box of smaller rocks, and began slipping them into the cracks and the crannies between the large rocks; he totally emptied the box of smaller rocks. Again, he asked if the jar was full now, and most of us took the bait again and said "yes." Then, he brought out a bowl of sand,

and as we all laughed at being tricked, he emptied the sand into the jar, too. "Now, is it totally full?" There was some hesitation this time, but most of us could not see any room for more rocks, sand, or anything, so we hesitantly said yes once more. Again, without saying anything, he pulled out his final container - a gallon of water - and he easily poured the whole gallon into the "completely full" jar. There may be several morals to this story, but one for sure is: *don't make up your mind too quickly.* Another would be: much more can fit into . . . an hour, a small car, a closet, a purse, a suitcase, a toy chest . . . or even a jar… than you might think at first glance.

WHAT IS THE MEANING TO YOU?

There is a story of two boys who were told they could have whatever was behind the door in front of each of them. The first boy opened his door and saw the room was full of money. He backed off, crossed his arms, and got a sad face. When asked, he stated, "With this much money, my dad says there's got to be an IRS agent close by." When the second boy opened his door, he found a room full of manure. He started grinning, and immediately began digging in the manure. When he was questioned, he stated, "With this much manure, there must be a pony close by." It all depends on your **perspective;** that is what determines the meaning of events.

THE BEST DECISION MAY BE TO WAIT AND SEE

A farmer reported to the local sheriff that his prize bull was mysteriously missing. The sheriff asked if the farmer wished to have a notice put out to try to find his bull. "No," said the farmer, "Let's not mention it to anyone and wait to see what happens." As the story goes, several months later, the farmer's neighbor ran into him at the feed store and asked if he ever found out what happened to his missing bull. The farmer simply replied, "Not until just now."

WE ALL STRUGGLE WITH INTERNAL CONFLICTS

One day, a woman sitting on her front porch noticed that her 5-year-old neighbor walked past her house. She thought this was somewhat odd, but let it go. About five minutes later, he walked by again, in the same direction, and she noticed that he had a determined look on his face. When he came by the third time, she rushed out to see if something was wrong. When she asked him if he was ok, he replied, "I'm running away from home." When she questioned him about walking by three times, he admitted quickly, "Well, I'm not allowed to cross the street."

HOW TO HANDLE NEIGHBORS

Once upon a time, there were three neighbors. One day the neighbor on one end came to the man in the middle house to warn him that his other neighbor was stealing firewood from his pile. The middle neighbor promised to take care of it. Several weeks later, the same neighbor on the end came to the middle neighbor and asked what had happened with the firewood problem. The neighbor in the middle simply said, "My other neighbor will never steal from me again. I told him if he ever needs firewood again, to come and get as much as he needs."

SIMILES

PEOPLE ARE LIKE BATTERIES, AND NEED TO RECHARGE

When I was in college, I had an older car that did well for me most of the time. But once in a while I would not close the door completely or forget to turn off the overhead light, and then leave it for the night. In the morning, the battery was "dead," and needed to be re-charged before it would work again. In those days, I took it out of the car, carried it to the local gas station, and left it for three hours to get the necessary re-charge. Then, I could take it back - four blocks, up-hill both ways - and start my car.

In our society, people think they are the Energizer® Bunny - they can go and go and go, never needing to stop or recharge. For years, this has been basically demanded from mothers, who are expected to balance jobs with laundry, shopping, meal preparation, and chauffeuring, as best they can. The idea of a break or a rest was usually out of the question. "Mothers are expected to just-keep-going. Others do it, why can't I?" Clearly, this is not a reasonable expectation for mothers or anyone else: **we all need time to re-charge every day.** This is true especially when we are totally run down or when there is more than the usual going on. There are times when recharging becomes our number one priority. We need to find and do those things that make us feel good and renew our energy, things like reading a good book, taking a long bath, going for a slow walk around the block, calling a friend, or listening to good music. Remember: let yourself re-charge – you need it.

PEOPLE ARE A LOT LIKE BALLOONS

Do you remember as a child playing with balloons? If you blew the balloon up just a little, you could squeeze it, push your finger all the way through it, smash it down almost flat, and pinch it in the middle to make two balloons. But, if you blew it up more, you had to be careful, because being rough with it would definitely make it

171

pop. Then, if you blew it up even more, you had to be extremely careful, since even brushing it on a smooth surface might pop it. Fortunately, letting some air out made that balloon pliable and playable again.

Stress does the same thing to people. When we have a little stress or strain in our lives, we can cope and be flexible enough to handle bumps along the road and outside pressure. But, as we fill up more with tension and stress, we "blow" more easily and our coping declines greatly. Then, if we take on even more stress, willingly or accidentally, almost anything can set us off, even the smallest demand, or change, or challenge. Fortunately, like with the balloon, if we **let off some pressure before we blow**, we become more flexible and able to cope. The trick is to **notice when we are "full up,"** so we can use our stress management tools to take off some of the pressure, just like with the balloon.

PEOPLE CAN BE A LOT LIKE SUPER-SATURATED SOLUTIONS

In a college chemistry class, I learned about the phenomenon of "super-saturated solutions." We were instructed to dissolve sugar in a beaker of water, then slowly add more sugar until we had to really stir to get it to dissolve. At this point, after lots of sugar was added, the water was still completely clear. Then we were instructed to scratch the inside of the beaker with our glass stirring rod. Well, sugar quickly sank to the bottom. If we stirred hard again, the sugar disappeared. Then, with a simple scratch of the stirring rod, some sugar again dropped to the bottom. Interesting, eh?

I believe the same "phenomenon" occurs with people: we can get too full and try to "hold" more than we can. At those times, we are apparently able to hold all the stress, tension, pressure, and challenges, and we keep going, trying to keep up. Then some little "scratch" disrupts the balance we held so precariously, and we lose it. It might be traffic that is the extra stressor which sets people off, especially when they are already "saturated" from their day at work. Then, the precarious balance fails. Grief can be that way, too, where people contain their feelings well, until a particular song, a familiar-sounding voice, or an oft-visited restaurant comes on their radar. Then, all the sugar (feelings) goes to the bottom.

PEOPLE ARE A LOT LIKE PRESSURE COOKERS

It is common knowledge that pressure cookers prepare food faster because of pressure - the pressure is a good thing. But, if the pressure is not released now and then, by the wobbly piece on top, the cooker could explode. I have heard people describe weeks of clean-up when this happens. Well, in people, pressure or stress builds up, too, and in some ways, that pressure is helpful to energize us and keep us going. But, at those times when we do not notice there is too much pressure, we are surprised when we "blow." We are aware pressure builds up in each of us, but we may not be aware how *much* is building up or how quickly. We may be too involved in our daily schedule to pay attention, and our automatic "wobbler" is not working (whatever that may be for us). The old story – about the man who came home from work and kicked the dog – is about *not realizing* how much pressure has built up. All of us would be better off if we had a gauge to help us know when we need to let off steam. That would help us function at our peak, *and* keep us from blowing our top.

PEOPLE ARE LIKE ONIONS

In psychotherapy, people often begin with one certain concern, which they are able to address adequately after a time in therapy. But, what often happens is another concern then arises - like peeling an onion. It is as if clearing away the first issue allowed this new one to show through. This can happen several times, with each "layer" becoming more difficult to handle, but clearly needing to be addressed.

I once worked with a couple who had anger issues, which they resolved. Then, they identified communication difficulties, which they addressed successfully, too. Then, they struggled to solve problems together, and got better. Finally, they got stuck on their biggest one - *trust*. In particular, he did not believe she was capable of correctly parenting a child, so he refused to have children with her. Because of her frustration, they divorced. Partly out of spite and partly to prove to herself she could, she had a baby on her own (sort of, you know) and began rearing it on her own terms. Surprisingly, after a while, the ex-husband started hanging around, and eventually they renewed their relationship. They are now raising the child together. They definitely peeled back a number of layers and ultimately were successful in dealing with the deepest and toughest: they created a workable relationship.

PEOPLE ARE A LOT LIKE A FROG IN A POT

Another therapist provided this metaphor, because it worked well for her in explaining our typical response to stress. According to scientists, if a frog is placed in a pot of water and the water is heated slowly, the frog will die in the pot as the water starts to boil. But, if a frog is placed into a pot of hot or boiling water, it will quickly hop out - saving its life. People in stressful situations are like that. If the stress has built slowly over a number of years, they are likely to stay in the situation, even though the stress "is killing them." But if the same person were placed into the situation when the stress is already high, most people would quickly leave. Unfortunately, this first situation describes many people in bad marriages or abusive jobs, where they may stay because the stress built slowly over time. If they "feel the heat" at all, they may seek therapy before the stress really kills them.

PEOPLE ARE A LOT LIKE VOLCANOES

We know volcanic eruptions result from a buildup of pressure and heat under the surface of the earth. When it builds enough, there can be an explosion as well as a flow of hot lava. Some people let problems simmer until they cannot hold the pressure any more. At that point, "they explode," spewing unexpected amounts of emotional steam and overflowing with a flow of feelings for some time afterward. We cannot stop volcanoes, but we *can* catch our own buildup of stress and pressure – and find a safe "vent" for relieving the pressure.